PRIVATE GARDENS
of PHILADELPHIA

PRIVATE GARDENS
of PHILADELPHIA

NICOLE JUDAY

Photographs by ROB CARDILLO

Gibbs Smith

CONTENTS

INTRODUCTION

Humans have been altering nature—for better or worse—for as long as we've existed as a species. Across most of that time, food, medicine, and raw materials were the primary goals of plant cultivation. But at some point in our ancient history people began growing plants not only for their useful qualities but also for their beauty, and arranging these beautiful plants in combinations that pleased the senses.

The Philadelphia region is home to an astonishing number of excellent gardens, both public and private. What are the specific circumstances or elements that created this intense concentration of horticulture? And why are there also so many ancillary organizations like plant societies, garden clubs, flower shows, and specialty nurseries? In the many delightful hours spent researching and visiting the gardens shown in this book and talking to their owners, I found some possible answers to these questions.

Ecologically, southeastern Pennsylvania has many enviable advantages that make it a particularly satisfying place to garden. The soil is generally friable with high organic matter, and the slightly acidic Ph is good for growing many types of ornamental plants. In most years rainfall is adequate and there are abundant sources of naturally occurring water. Since Philadelphia is known as the "northernmost Southern city and the southernmost Northern city," the climate allows us to grow an incredibly diverse number of species that would be impossible in areas that are just a bit colder or warmer. And the landscape itself is naturally attractive, if less often dramatic. Located on the geologically oldest part of the continent, the land has few sharp edges and almost no flat areas, but instead offers mellow, undulating contours. Interesting rock and water features lend themselves to enhancement, and perhaps to the temporary fantasy of being tamable by the human hand.

There are reasons besides ecology that make Philadelphia the nucleus for gardening in America, some of which go back to the city's origins in the late 1600s. Envisioned by founder William Penn as a "greene country towne," his original plan incorporated five large squares devoted to public green space, four of which still survive more than 300 years later. Quakers were the dominant order in early Philadelphia, but soon the city attracted other settlers fleeing religious persecution in Europe. These included sects of mystics who found their spiritual homes in nature rather than in church, and who established the first known botanical garden in America.

Generations later, this same deep connection with nature and the study of its mysteriously intricate systems has made Philadelphia the most important American city in the burgeoning field of natural history. Based upon the close observation of nature rather than laboratory experimentation, natural history includes the discipline of botany, and plants from around the world began coming to and through Philadelphia for study and collection. The Pennsylvania Horticultural Society, founded in 1827, helped facilitate the exchange of knowledge about plants. It also established cash incentives for its members to find or develop ornamental and edible plants that would be well-suited to the conditions of southeastern Pennsylvania, resulting in the introduction of many superior varieties throughout the nineteenth century.

In addition to the scientists and mystics, another group contributed to this region's early horticultural prominence—millionaires. Although it lost the distinction long ago, in the late nineteenth and early twentieth centuries Philadelphia was very, very rich. This was largely due to the incredible natural resources exploited throughout the state of Pennsylvania. In terms of outsized wealth, fin de siècle Philadelphia was analogous to Silicon Valley today—a place where advances in technology allowed massive fortunes to be made with jaw-dropping speed. The region's coal, steel, and railroad tycoons found ways to extract and monetize the vast deposits of high-quality coal and iron that lay under the ground throughout much of Pennsylvania. These industries were fueled by charcoal made from the hardwood trees covering the entirety of the state, which could burn hot enough to melt iron ore and refine small amounts of steel. The steel was used to lay the thousands of miles of railroad track necessary for transporting coal from the mines to cities up and down the Eastern seaboard and for revolutionizing transportation, another lucrative industry. With these ingredients, plus regular infusions of immigrant labor from southern and eastern Europe—treated as another cheap and exploitable commodity—fortunes were made the likes of which Philadelphia had not previously known.

These titans of industry, or more often their wives, created amazing gardens. English, French, or Italianate in style, the gardens were spared no expense, with the owners ordering massive amounts of earth to be moved, often by hand, for the creation of terraces, loggias, grottos, fountains, cascades, gazebos, formal walled gardens, iris bowls, woodland gardens, and every other type of garden feature they or their landscape architects could dream up. Appropriately for an era predicated upon the presumption of omnipotence, everything was built to last forever.

Perhaps to compensate for the less-than-genteel origins of fortunes made by the dirty, dangerous work of underpaid labor, newly wealthy Philadelphians also became enamored with recreating the trappings of old-money English country life. Sports like foxhunting and cricket as well as gentlemen farming became fashionable, earning Philadelphia a reputation for being eccentrically Anglophilic. It must have required some juggling for early industrialists to run their businesses while keeping up a strict appearance of leisure that required fox hunting three days a week. This legacy of simulated English country life is still evident in the preserved farms and open spaces close to Philadelphia, and in the gardens that remain on a few of them.

Most of the grand estates and replica English country homes from this era lasted only decades before being razed or subdivided. After World War II, even the wealthiest Philadelphians' appetite waned for properties requiring an army of staff to operate and mountains of coal to heat. But enough remain, mostly in fragments, to maintain a link to a time when gardening was not just a hobby but was considered a social necessity and an acceptably gracious manner for displaying one's affluence. While most of the people featured in this book have no personal connection to the golden age of Philadelphia gardens (although some do) there are certainly indirect influences, not the least of which are the public gardens like Longwood, Chanticleer, and Morris Arboretum that were once beautifully gardened private estates and today offer inspiration and ideas to gardeners with all levels of experience. Many garden clubs and plant societies that emerged during this time still nurture the pursuit of greater horticultural knowledge and foster community among gardeners, which, along with our incredible nurseries, encourage anyone with a spark of curiosity to pursue the interest.

The outdoor spaces in this book represent a more intensive approach to gardening than many would care to undertake, because gardening at this level requires a serious commitment. The beautiful scenes here may look almost effortlessly natural, but they are products of years, or in many cases decades, of hard physical labor and financial trade-offs, not to mention responding to repeated existential threats from tornados, floods, deer, unwanted development, and unanticipated acts of nature. Each of these gardens, including the most elaborate, also exists despite some combination of constraints—an unattractive or obstructed view, traffic noises, or challenging light and climate conditions. But this is the secret that all gardeners know: constraints are necessary to push one's limits of resourcefulness and creativity and to cultivate something extraordinary.

The gardens we are sharing here were created by people with a wide range of personal backgrounds, places of origin, careers, and life experiences. Yet besides their collective passion for gardening, many of their stories have surprisingly similar themes. Most of these gardeners started with a blank slate. Even more often, at the time they were acquired, the properties had been through some previous degradation that required

herculean effort to reverse. In story after story gardeners recalled removing thickets of noxious plants, remediating depleted soil, fixing drainage issues, and restoring natural waterways before a thought could be given to putting plants in the ground.

The other, quite touching theme among our gardeners is around generational memories. Many people talked about how their love of gardening developed early on from family and extended relatives, even if they didn't know it at the time. A mother in Illinois who allowed her teenage son to rip up the front yard to plant a vegetable garden. A grandmother whose Victory Garden in Pittsburgh was cultivated to help feed seven children, who then also became gardeners. Recollections of a rural Pennsylvania childhood with a mother who was fascinated by trees; aunts who would come over to plant roses; a grandfather who would carefully polish a freshly picked pear before bestowing it on a child. These and many other vivid reminiscences, almost none of which found their way into the final chapters, speak to how well gardens can foster meaningful interactions between people, and how effective they are at nurturing the legacy of a family, a community, a city.

As a dependable rule, gardeners are extremely generous. They are quick to share plants, provide advice and encouragement, loan tools, and help with hard labor. Most gardeners are spurred by the desire for what they've created to be enjoyed by others—friends, family, or just passersby. The people who have graciously shared their gardens for this book help to make this infectious culture of generosity even more durable. We hope that readers will feel this spirit in its pages and be inspired to pass it on.

A GARDEN
ON EVERY LEVEL

Gladwyne

When the last remaining fragment of an early nineteenth-century working farm in Gladwyne was purchased thirty years ago, the large parcel had just been subdivided, foretelling the demise of its rural identity. Goodbye, solitary fieldstone farmhouse, whose front door, for practical purposes, marked the end of an arrow-straight farm lane. In short order, the property began a new chapter as the last house on a suburban cul-de-sac.

While the change to a typical greensward was dramatic, a series of bold—and, at times, topographically defiant—architectural and horticultural interventions have since transformed the property's outdoors yet again—this time into an unexpected fantasy garden that weaves together the design traditions of Italy, France, and England. Today, multiple garden spaces—most separated by formal hedges and elevation changes and employing old-world design concepts, materials, and objects—reference an antiquity almost never recreated on this side of the Atlantic.

The perfectly flat approach to the house is deceiving, as the building is situated at the property's highest point, and the ground declines steeply behind it. To make this backyard usable, the hillside has been excavated and sculpted over time to create five separate levels, each utilizing similar design elements. Perfectly clipped hornbeam, linden, and beech hedges help evoke a cloistered feel in various spaces; axial walks create a sense of depth; and carefully placed garden accents, planters, and water features serve as focal points. Not surprising is the fact that the garden, overseen during its development by garden designer Chuck Gale, took more than a decade to complete. But given the perfect symmetry and balance between the individual elements and the whole, it is surprising—and a tribute to the designer's vision—that these changes were made without the assistance of a master plan.

The first part of the property that Gale tackled was a flat side lawn that he converted into a classic English-style double mixed border. The wide space, visible from the screened-in porch, is anchored by a large panicle hydrangea in each of its four corners and planted with brightly colored spring bulbs, which are followed by a succession of vibrant annuals and perennials that provide vivid color throughout the seasons.

Cut into the hillside below is a walled tennis court, covered in grass rather than a hard surface due to the area's fragile watershed and

local restrictions on impervious surfaces. On the banks above the court, blossoms of everblooming roses appear like thousands of spectators with their heads turned in expectation that at any moment the next match will begin. An antique zinc-covered garden gazebo imported from Europe, which serves as storage for tennis equipment, completes this picture of gentility.

A level down from the court, a Callery pear allée creates a shaded walkway. Underneath, bricks set in a diamond pattern are spaced perfectly to receive human-scaled footfalls. A central landing is punctuated by four symmetrical stone spheres and the all-seeing eye of a crystal orb. High above, a boxwood-lined terrace behind the house contains beds of roses underplanted with English lavender. Various seating areas exploit views of the swimming pool, which is reached by a set of twin staircases ornamented by Second Empire–style metal balustrades.

In the entrance courtyard, where newer construction is nearby, the challenge was to provide a visual separation that didn't clash with the neighboring buildings. This was achieved by creating a square, walled-in entrance yard screened from the road by a deep hedge and edged with antique bricks. The courtyard's centerpiece is a saucer magnolia, chosen for its multiple trunks that, when peered through, make the space feel deeper and larger than it really is. A mature zelkova stands sentinel in each corner, repeating the symmetrical motif seen in other parts of the garden.

Throughout the landscape, the formal design elements are enhanced by an array of antique garden ornaments, from a classic French courtyard fountain made of limestone to quirkier pieces like a nineteenth-century wine barrel scale. A monumental urn from the 1920s placed at the center of a Victorian-style garden bedded in a red-and-white checkerboard pattern, invokes a vision of the Queen of Hearts imperiously marching from behind the sheared beech hedge to threaten a game of croquet.

Due to the exacting cultural and maintenance demands required, there are very few existing examples of the formal European-style gardens popularized during the nineteenth and early twentieth century's golden age of horticulture, when wealthy Americans brought ideas and objects back from their European travels at a time when antiquities were inexpensive, labor was cheap, highly skilled (often European-trained) gardeners were plentiful, and manure was everywhere. To find a contemporary garden that hews so carefully to the romantic traditions of this demanding and almost forsaken design style is remarkable. The faithfulness with which this vision has been carried out elevates this garden from being a curiosity to a convincing fantasy, conjuring a world that may exist only in our imaginations.

PRECEDING OVERLEAF: An oversized urn from the 1920s is the focal point of the checkerboard garden, planted with alternating squares of red, white, and purple annuals.

OPPOSITE: Antique paving bricks impart an old-world elegance to the boxwood-and-lavender-lined terrace garden overlooking the pool.

PRECEDING OVERLEAF: An exterior view of the vaulted arched gazebo, flanked by a double row of mophead hydrangeas and espaliered Kousa dogwoods. ABOVE: The outdoor dining area showing steps leading up to the house. OPPOSITE TOP LEFT: The owners are fond of antique water features like this fountain. OPPOSITE TOP RIGHT: A multistemmed magnolia is the focal point of the courtyard entrance. OPPOSITE BOTTOM LEFT: Roses overlook the grass tennis court. OPPOSITE BOTTOM RIGHT: Zinc containers are filled with seasonal annuals.

PRECEDING OVERLEAF: An outdoor sitting area with a view up to the tennis court. Spheres are a repeating motif in the garden, which is laid out along regular axes and adheres to symmetrical design. ABOVE: The metal railings of the stone steps leading from the path to the pool were repurposed from an 1870s Philadelphia building. RIGHT: An antique clock face graces the outdoor pizza oven. OPPOSITE TOP: An allée of Callery pears. OPPOSITE BELOW: Although identical in appearance, the structure on the right is a dining area, while the left hides a hot tub. The garden contains hundreds of boxwoods, all of which are clipped regularly.

DEEPLY ROOTED

Wayne

When Caren Lambert decided to build on the three-acre property she had purchased in Wayne, Pennsylvania, she envisioned a home constructed at the top of a pleasing rise and overlooking gardens that would create a strong connection to the outdoors. The daughter and granddaughter of avid gardeners, she had lived in many other places, including Florida, California, and several years in Russia, but had never had a garden that felt like her own. Designing a home and garden in tandem gave her the opportunity to put down roots for her family in every sense.

Careful consideration was given to how the home—a Queen Anne–style Victorian, similar to many others nearby—would relate to its surroundings and tie in with the outdoors. Living spaces—designed with plenty of curtainless windows—are filled with natural light and have wide views out into the landscape. The all-white paint scheme (both indoors and out) serves as a foil for the colorful beauty of the garden.

Good gardeners know how valuable it is to work within constraints. The need to work with or against limiting factors, whether it's terrible soil, difficult terrain, or a tight budget, is often the starting point for the most interesting gardens. In the case of Lambert's property, the primary hurdle was excessive stormwater runoff resulting from a combination of poor-draining clay soil and the proximity of two small streams that feed directly into nearby Fenimore Pond. The homeowner realized that building a large home on the property would reduce the amount of open ground available to soak up rainfall, meaning more water would run off during heavy rains into streams whose banks were already badly eroded.

The solution was a series of rain gardens designed by landscape architect Jonathan Alderson. While these water features look natural, they are actually highly engineered and precisely constructed using specially engineered highly absorbent soil that was brought in to replace the poor-draining soil native to the site. A sequence of swales following the natural contours of the land were excavated at critical areas to capture the most water possible. During rainstorms, water courses into these depressions, which are linked by a system of underground pipes that distribute water to soak in evenly. Instead of running off into the streams and causing more erosion, the captured water discharges slowly back into the ground.

Even more water is taken up by the roots of the native perennials, trees, and shrubs that were chosen for their ability to tolerate both boggy conditions and hot, dry spells in summer. Swamp cypress, river birch, and sweetbay magnolia trees make up the largest mass in the rain gardens, and each specimen can absorb up to 150 gallons of water per day, later transpiring this moisture through its foliage. Shrubs like buttonbush, winterberry holly, chokeberry, American beautyberry, Virginia sweetspire, and clethra secure the banks of the depressions. Filling in the gaps are tough perennials such as Joe Pye weed, bee balm, obedient plant, and various asters and amsonias that require little maintenance and outcompete any emerging weed seeds, as well as support the larval stage of many pollinators and serve nectar and pollen to adults. Besides slowing the flow of water into the streams, the system of rain gardens also acts as a giant filter, removing pollutants before runoff enters the waterways. As with any filter, the rain gardens work best when kept free-flowing and unclogged, so all plant debris is meticulously removed at the end of the growing season.

To further mitigate stormwater runoff, large areas of lawn—which has a limited ability to soak up water due to its shallow root system—were converted to meadow. Warm-season grasses such as big bluestem, little bluestem, and cultivars of panicum, as well as deep-rooted meadow perennials like baptisias, eryngiums, and echinaceas, thrive in soil that's been kept intentionally lean with little added organic matter, which has the advantage of limiting competition from other plants needing more nutrients. Lambert was skeptical when Alderson assured her that a meadow could supply a screen that would offer privacy and block the view of passing cars, but within a few years, the plantings had fulfilled that promise. As an added plus, the meadow requires cutting back only once a year (in late winter), a considerable labor savings over the regular mowing required for turf.

Other areas of the garden are designed within the overall naturalistic aesthetic but incorporate different design elements and an expanded plant palette. Off the back of the house, multiple parterres featuring repeated plantings of coppiced smokebush trees underplanted with alliums and salvias provide a dramatic architectural counterpoint to the tapestry-like meadow plantings. A protected corner outside the kitchen door creates a favorable microclimate for less cold-hardy plants like camellias. Also at home here is a sentimental collection of the old-fashioned "memory plants" that Lambert associates with Philadelphia, including lily of the valley, assorted columbines, and a weeping willow. On a lower level, a boxwood-lined walled garden frames a rectangle of lawn left open for entertaining and recreation.

A few years after her home and garden were completed, Lambert had the opportunity to purchase an adjacent three-acre parcel. Having become enamored with the sensitive ecosystem

PRECEDING OVERLEAF: Fall is the most glorious season in this garden, where native species of shrubs and perennials intermingle under the autumn foliage of an ornamental cherry tree.

OPPOSITE: A sheltered area behind the house encourages the proliferation of spreading perennials such as pink evening primrose and sedum, which find their way into the cracks between bluestone pavers.

she had created around her house, she was drawn to the idea of doing further ecological service by restoring the new property in a similar way. Here, a few existing pockets of native trout lilies have expanded under her care, and a seeded meadow is taking hold. She is supplementing this new area with extra self-sown plants taken from her original mature garden. Dogwoods, for example, that were planted there ten years ago are now producing seedlings, and she carefully transplants them to the new meadow, tucking them in so that they can put down deep and lasting roots, just as she has.

LEFT: Royal Purple smokebushes are coppiced each spring to maintain their shape and vibrant foliage. The purple tones are picked up by salvia and allium in the garden's sole formal border. OVERLEAF: One of the property's rain gardens, planted with moisture-tolerant shrubs such as winterberry hollies, whose berries provide winter forage for birds. The warm-season grasses screen the property from the nearby road and help slow the flow of stormwater into the adjacent creek.

OPPOSITE: A shady nook planted with ferns and native mayapples, which spread happily in the right conditions. THIS PAGE: 1. Deep rooted baptisia in the meadow. 2. Native Indian grass. 3. Boxwood lining the walled cutting garden. 4. Seedpod of southern magnolia. 5. Native buttonbush thrives in wet soils and is planted throughout the rain gardens. 6. Sea oats growing with the fall-fruiting beautyberry bush. 7. A multistemmed river birch shows off its peeling, textural bark. 8. Tubular flowers like those of the obedient plant attract pollinators throughout the season.

ROSES
AND RUINS

Haverford

No region of Pennsylvania has a stronger connection to the Gilded Age of American architecture and landscape design than the Main Line. The area was named after the Pennsylvania Railroad line built across the William Penn–assigned Welsh Tract, a swath of farms and mills underpopulated until the Civil War. By the late nineteenth century, rail service had made the Main Line easily accessible from Philadelphia. It quickly became the most desirable location for prosperous Philadelphians to establish properties and lifestyles that were rural yet cultivated, simulating the rustic elegance of English country life replete with requisite old-world pastimes like cricket and foxhunting.

One of the first of the large estates to be established on the Main Line was Cheswold, the summer residence of Alexander J. Cassatt, president of the Pennsylvania Railroad. A huge figure during his lifetime, he was responsible for (among other accomplishments) the creation of rail tunnels under the Hudson River and the construction of Pennsylvania Station in New York City. Today, his historical significance is eclipsed by that of his sister, the impressionist painter Mary Cassatt.

Cheswold, finished in 1872, was a hulking Queen Anne–style villa with Gothic overtones, in essence an advertisement for the Main Line itself. But like many of the first generation of Main Line mansions built to showcase new wealth, the house was so large that it soon outlived its usefulness. It had been empty for some time before catching fire, and it was ultimately demolished in the 1930s. This anticlimactic ending of one era sowed the seeds for the next, bringing us to the garden of Reggie and Frank Thomas, whose 1.2-acre property sits quite literally on the ruins of the Cheswold estate.

The Thomases had decided to relocate their young family from Center City in the mid-1980s and purchased a Walter Durham–built home in a 1940s Haverford development. The house was situated on a "flag lot," set behind the other homes in the neighborhood with only a narrow strip of land wide enough for a driveway extending to the street. At first, it was like living in a fishbowl. "We were in the middle of seven houses," recalls Reggie, and all were visible from the home and property. Designed in a somewhat English and somewhat French style, the rambling cottage was placed just above the point where the property begins descending to the valley of Mill Creek below.

When the Thomases moved in, they saw beyond the property's deficits—some awkward lines in the home's design, its lack of natural light, an oversized asphalt parking area that brought cars almost to the living room window, and the complete absence of a garden. Instead, they focused on the advantages, including some beautiful Cassatt-era hardwood trees and a tabula rasa upon which to create the garden of Reggie's pent-up dreams, one bursting with colorful flowers and intoxicating fragrance. Until then, she had made do with container gardens and window boxes in her tiny city garden, but in this new space, she was able to set her sights on something much more ambitious.

Little did she and Frank know how much determination would be needed to bring their vision of a romantic Eden to reality. In almost every place they dug, they hit chunks of Cheswold, unearthing stone walls and even colossal chimneys beneath the soil's surface. One of the first tasks was to design a welcoming entrance garden, and the large, meticulously dressed stones used to give the garden its courtyard-like appearance were pulled straight from the ground. A short time later, a bed of roses was unknowingly planted over a buried slate walkway, ruining the drainage and requiring a summer to remove the soil and chip out the slate before putting the bed back together again.

It took decades, but working together, the Thomases eventually conquered the remaining relics of a monument that had been constructed to convey omnipotence and to withstand the ages. Today, no visible signs of their epic struggle remain. The home, which has been improved by the addition of larger windows and the planting of climbing hydrangeas and roses to soften its walls, serenely overlooks a rose garden that Reggie has cultivated to perfection. It's framed by a charmingly domestic white picket fence, beckoning visitors into the space and offering vertical support for Frank's favorite clematis vines.

After guests pass through the rose garden, a classic arbor twined with roses leads them down a set of stone steps to a swimming pool. Earth removed during the pool's construction had been banked behind low stone walls, and these new beds were planted with more roses as well as stalwart perennials like Hosta sieboldii and lamb's ears. Everywhere, sweeps of repeating perennials and color-coordinated bulbs help maintain an atmosphere of tranquility. This style evolved due to necessity, Reggie recalls. "In the earliest days, the cheapest way to get more plants was to divide and divide and divide and divide and divide." But the aesthetic still compels her, as the repetition of colors, textures, and shapes gives the gardens a sense of harmony and unity.

Behind the house, a large flagstone patio enclosed within low stone walls overlooks a sloping lawn, which ends at the edge of a tree canopy.

PRECEDING OVERLEAF: The gateless entrance to the rose garden sends a subtle signal that all are welcome.

OPPOSITE: A garden arch festooned with the classic Constance Spry climbing rose leads from the rose garden down to the pool area.

The lush vegetation makes the property very private but took many years to become effective at doing so. When the first of their daughters married, the Thomases installed a series of grassy steps, which were secured by Belgian-block risers and led down to the bottom of the lawn where the ceremony was held. The project posed some obstacles (including, of course, more Cheswold remains discovered when they started digging), but when the steps were finally completed, they connected the family with a part of the landscape that had previously been rarely utilized. A vintage pergola and simple table and chairs now draw the Thomases to the spot, where they can look up and enjoy the fullness of what they've created.

Far from being battle weary, the Thomases actually look back fondly on the many years of effort required to vanquish the vestiges of Cheswold and make a garden that is entirely their own. Perhaps the most gratifying outcome of their shared passion and sustained determination is that their children now bring their own children to enjoy many extended family weekends at the peaceful oasis that has emerged like a phoenix from the ashes of another era.

LEFT: Bright pink Country Dancer shrub roses take center stage while the paler climbing Sea Foam and Dr. Van Fleet roses soften the home's stucco walls. OVERLEAF LEFT: Stone steps flanked by a double hedge of barberry descend from the rose garden to the pool area, whose perennial beds are mostly propagated by division. OVERLEAF RIGHT: The delicate blossoms of Clematis montana grace an antique wrought-iron trellis.

LEFT: This rose, which long ago lost its plant tag, eventually found its own way to a nearby paperbark maple, where it has grown ever since. ABOVE: Roses planted with perennial companions catmint and lamb's ears. RIGHT: The large-flowering clematis Rebecca clambers up a picket fence. OVERLEAF: The cottage aesthetic extends to the back patio, once visible from neighboring homes. Today, it's a private oasis screened by a backdrop of mature trees.

NATURE
AND NURTURE

Coatesville

The farthest reach of a Philadelphia collar county is just a few minutes from where horse-drawn buggies of the Pennsylvania Dutch begin sharing the roads with trucks and cars. Located in the Brandywine Valley, southeastern Chester County still retains the rural character and agricultural heritage of centuries past and contains more continuous, preserved open space than almost any other part of the region.

This land hasn't remained so undeveloped by happenstance. Farm upon farm began being acquired more than one hundred years ago by foxhunters who found their ability to run the hounds closer to Philadelphia hampered by development. As cultivated fields were replaced with grass and pasture, and barbed wire fencing was switched for post and rail (better for jumping), an aesthetic evolved that was both beautiful and optimal for riding. Today the area is still used by the Cheshire Hunt, one of several such clubs that remain in the region.

Lured by the open landscape, wealthy Philadelphians—particularly equestrians—came to the region to establish country estates. Such was the draw for Sir John Thouron, one of the most eminent characters in twentieth-century horticulture. The upper-crust Scot and his DuPont heiress wife purchased a large farm they named Doe Run, after the pretty stream that wends its way through its eponymous valley, so she could ride and he could make a garden, one that became famous during his lifetime. Ultimately spanning around twenty acres of the five-hundred-acre estate, the densely cultivated garden islands he created amid extensive lawns surrounded an old farmhouse, parts of which dated back to the eighteenth century. Among the cultivated spaces were an alpine garden that was considered one of the best in the country, a seventy-five-foot double perennial border planted against an immense sheared hemlock hedge, and another garden planted around a collection of rare conifers.

Thouron built large greenhouses to provide cut flowers for the home, and when he and his wife traveled, boxes of fresh Doe Run flowers would be airmailed to them twice a week. A fervent collector, he corresponded with plant experts and explorers from around the world to acquire slips, cuttings, and seeds of the rarest specimens, at one point cultivating a row of pink-blooming dandelions that he had gone to great lengths to obtain.

A gardening staff was retained to maintain the property to Thouron's exacting standards, and generations of horticulturists, some recruited from ads placed in Scottish newspapers, developed the grounds. When the prominent horticulturist died at age ninety-nine in 2007, a few of the staff stayed on, keeping watch over the gardens while the property awaited its next chapter.

The current owners purchased the property in 2010 and later bought several more farms to bring its current size to around eight hundred acres. As business executives who are also intensely creative, they had long been drawn to the idea of farming and had been searching for the right property for some time. For two years before moving in, they oversaw renovations on two dozen buildings and completed a variety of new construction projects throughout the property.

The old greenhouses near the main house were demolished, and three recycled commercial greenhouses were erected farther away to frame a one-acre vegetable garden. Here, dozens of raised beds grow large quantities of nearly every fruit and vegetable that can be cultivated in southeastern Pennsylvania. Reminiscent of the great walled gardens in England, this protected space contains a tunnel of espaliered apples, rows of peach trees and berry beds, as well as sections reserved for flowers, herbs, and medicinal plants. On the hillside beyond, cows can be seen placidly grazing in the pastures. These cows, along with sheep and goats, produce milk for the farm's most

well-known activity, an award-winning cheese-making operation. But the vegetable gardeners claim that the livestock are most valued for their manure, which is helping to increase the soil's fertility after decades of being cultivated for hay.

While the farmhouse and several other nearby buildings were also refashioned, most of the Thouron-era landscape was preserved. Some of these gardens, like the famous double border that lines up on a perfect axis with the home's front entrance, are tended much like they were during the time when the gentleman of the house would lead garden clubs through the property, stopping at plants to announce their Latin names. This story is among the recollections of several gardeners who have spent their entire careers at Doe Run Farm and still practice their craft according to the traditional, old-world training they received from Thouron, whose gardening practices are mostly extinct due to their laboriousness and reliance on extravagant amounts of greenhouse space.

Behind the house, which lies on a rise, a stone patio overlooks most of the gardens. A wide, fan-shaped stone stairway leading down to the lawn was designed with small openings for pockets of petite rock garden specimens, such as irises, phlox, columbines, and sedums, which bloom in waves throughout the spring and summer.

The original alpine garden was built on either side of a stream-like water feature that cascades down a series of large stones collected from around the farm. As the decades passed, the

PRECEDING OVERLEAF: Portions of the vegetable garden are set aside for perennials like these asters, used for arrangements, and edible flowers such as nasturtiums.

OPPOSITE: The eye-catching seed pods of the annual nigella.

OPPOSITE: A formal decorative urn contrasts with the simplicity of traditional farmhouse architecture. THIS PAGE: 1. One of the many pastures used for raising dairy animals. 2. The nodding blossoms of a bush clematis. 3. A whimsical fountain brings both sound and movement to a garden near the home. 4. Unfurling flower stems of astilbe poke through the foliage of nigella. 5. The flower stalks of red hot poker emerge in early summer. 6. Red-winged blackbirds are drawn to the open grasslands. 7. Mophead hydrangea in hanging baskets. 8. Italian Bugloss features tiny blue flowers upon tall stems.

ABOVE: Potted plants are kept in greenhouses and rotated in and out of the home. LEFT: Planted stone steps cascade from the patio to the yard. OPPOSITE TOP: The white garden in springtime. OPPOSITE BELOW: A sweeping, freestanding perennial border near one of the property's venerable Thouron-era beech trees. OVERLEAF: The plain architectural style of a renovated stable complements the informal mixed border of annuals and perennials.

ABOVE: A container of agapanthus in bud.
RIGHT: The same gardeners have tended the
perennial border for decades, often saving
seeds and taking cuttings to use the following
year. OVERLEAF LEFT: As the alpine garden
became shadier over time, the plantings
have also transitioned. In spring, the garden
is filled with columbines and primroses.
OVERLEAF RIGHT: A few of the many unusual
and dwarf conifer specimens, interplanted
with warm-season grasses and perennials like
coneflower.

background planting of mixed conifers matured, overwhelming and shading the sun-loving alpine species. Today, moisture-loving perennials like candelabra primroses, ferns, and mosses are nestled between the boulders in this garden and thrive in the damp shade. Rhododendron and other evergreen shrubs grow among the weathered rocks and evoke a sense of mystery beneath the curtain of conifers planted decades ago.

Other legacy spaces are similarly maintained to preserve their character but with a refreshed interpretation. In a combination of contrasting hues, shapes, and textures, dwarf conifers, Japanese maples, and other unusual trees are arranged on either side of a winding, dry stone bed that recalls the shape and appearance of a stream. Perennials such as salvias, echinaceas, and rudbeckias are interspersed with warm-season grasses, capturing light and creating movement against the static conifers.

Additional references to the Doe Run are plentiful. Sinuous paths and beds mimic the shape of natural waterways, and a set of curving stone steps are placed to emulate the way water flows down a creek bed. These steps lead to a sunken garden planted exclusively with white-flowered plants of various shapes and textures that gleam against the darker stone walls.

The Doe Run itself is now a primary focal point of the farm. The stream runs through the bottom of a former hay pasture, where decades of farm runoff and regular flooding in the valley had caused sediment buildup and degraded the creek's banks. Soon after the current owners acquired the farm, they began an ambitious project to restore one hundred acres of riparian land to how it was three hundred years ago. The pasture has now been converted into a meadow that, for maximum wildlife benefit, is never mowed. A dedicated gardener is gradually increasing the number of native trees, which is now up to around one hundred types, including magnolias, sweetgums, and sycamores that can tolerate some standing water. An extensive network of paths has been established, and every day the owners take walks through the meadows and along the Doe Run, stopping at various naturalistic seating areas that have been planted for their enjoyment with special combinations of showier native plants.

Everywhere on the farm, the owners' personal aesthetic is incorporated in sometimes subtle, sometimes explicit ways. They find great beauty in all of nature's expressions, even the cycle of decay. Dead trees are left up, their naked twisting forms standing out amid the lushness of the surroundings. New buildings are finished to look worn with age, and stains on stone walls are left unscrubbed. Despite all the cultivation and activity at Doe Run Farm, much of it quite complex, a sense prevails that these pursuits are always subordinate to nature and seek to harmonize with the land, rather than trying to bend nature's magnificence to the will of humans.

PRECEDING OVERLEAF: Cows graze peacefully in the pasture above the vegetable garden, which grows almost all of the family's produce.

OPPOSITE: An unmown verge of self-sowing annuals brightens the edge of a pasture.

ABOVE: Heavily coppicing coral bark willows in winter will result in more vibrant new growth in spring.
OPPOSITE: Beauty is everywhere, including in the weathered stump of an old willow that somehow still puts on new growth.

A GARDEN UNFINISHED

East Falls

For Suzanne Penn, the idea of a perfect garden is beside the point. Regularly outdoors by 5:30 a.m., she devotes her early hours to pruning, weeding, staking, or even moving a special plant just a few inches forward to give it a more favorable place to grow. She has spent the past thirty years gardening her small property in the East Falls section of Northwest Philadelphia, which was a blank canvas of turf when she began working on it. The passing decades have given her ample time to reflect on the evolution of the spaces and to study the way light changes throughout the seasons. Today, she keeps the garden beautifully tended—wild enough to create a sense of mystery, but with every plant precisely located to serve a specific aesthetic and functional purpose.

The snail's pace of progress in Penn's garden suits her. By profession she is a modern-art conservator, a career that she gravitated to from her own deep interest in and regard for the process of creating—the experience itself, not just a means to achieve the end goal of a finished product. "Ephemerality is a positive for me," she says, "which is funny, since my job is to make people's objects last forever." Besides gardening, she also enjoys making clothing, textiles, and ceramics

because the complexity and labor intensiveness of the work delays the moment when a project is finished and becomes static (and often to her mind, useless). Happily, the nature of gardening guarantees that no gardener, herself included, will ever actually complete a garden. Things always change.

Penn grew up in relatively seasonless California, and she appreciates the opportunity that the mid-Atlantic region gives her to annually reset the garden almost back to a start, precluding any risk of boredom-inducing stasis. During her early years living in a temperate climate, she developed a love of Mediterranean plants, which have proved to be relatively torturous to grow in her current, much-less-forgiving climate, where they need to be overwintered indoors. She has gradually weaned herself from the tender plants of her childhood, whittling her citrus collection down to just two specimens and forgoing many of the exotic plants that she still longs for. "Having a teeny garden means being absolutely ruthless about how you use your space," she notes. That tough-love philosophy has caused her to also give some nonnatives that have limited value to wildlife the heave-ho and has influenced her shift from collecting rare

71

and often fussy plants to those that perform well and are beautiful, even if they're not the most unusual species.

Penn's sophisticated eye has employed a series of visual tricks to transform the flat rectangle of her backyard into several different spaces, each with a beginning, an end, and a focal point. Just a single, sinuous pathway of grass remains from the original wall-to-wall carpet of lawn, and even this greensward cleverly becomes narrower to create the illusion of traversing into the distance. She has been inspired by illustrations of gardens in early-twentieth-century children's books, in which some plants ominously tower overhead while others are so tiny they require close-up, hands-and-knees investigation. "I love really big plants that almost feel menacing, and really small plants that you discover in nooks and crannies—and then only when you look very closely," she explains.

At no point is the entire garden visible; instead, a visitor navigates a circuitous route past imposing eight-foot Scheherazade oriental lilies and a Lilliputian grove of Jacquemontii birch trees, selected for their milk-white bark. The beds are dominated by saturated hues of deep reds, purples, and blues, and textures vary from the spikiness of castor beans to the velvetiness of lamb's ears. Penn currently favors chocolate cosmos for the long-lived beauty the plant brings to both the garden and arrangements, boasting deep reddish-brown blooms that appear almost black in certain light.

Besides color and texture, sound and movement also matter deeply here. The property fronts a busy city street, so several splashing water features near seating areas mask the noise of traffic and contribute to the garden's feeling of tranquility. Behind the house, a raised patio overlooks a large, naturalistic pond banked by Wissahickon schist, a local stone. The hue of the goldfish in the water here complements both the deep shade cast by a nearby Sunsation magnolia as well as its yellow flowers.

Choosing plants that attract pollinators ensures constant motion among the beds, from a fluttering swallowtail alighting on a butterfly bush to a slender lavender stem quivering under the weight of a honeybee. Fragrant plants foster a different kind of sensory experience, but Penn's allergies keep her from enjoying that to the fullest. "I do stop and smell the roses, and then I almost always regret it," she mourns.

A section of what was once the front lawn has been turned over to Penn's most recent gardening interest: growing flowers for cutting and adding into arrangements, many of which she displays in ceramic vases she makes for this purpose. In the past several years, she's become an expert at packing a profusion of cut-and-come-again annuals, such as gaillardias, scabiosas, zinnias, and bachelor's buttons, into this small space, where she also conducts an ongoing study of dahlias. Ever the researcher, she takes notes on her dahlias throughout the growing season, documenting

PRECEDING OVERLEAF: Although small, the garden generates maximum interest by mixing hardscaping materials, using a variety of decorative elements, and combining plants with contrasting colors and textures.

OPPOSITE: The larger of two ponds creates habitat, allows for the cultivation of unusual aquatic plants, and keeps the sounds of the city from intruding into the garden.

their specific cultural requirements as well as which plants are most floriferous and have the longest vase life. Her current top picks are boysenberry-hued Ivanetti and golden orange-flowered Sylvia. Those that don't meet her high bar for performance get the shovel treatment.

Despite the discipline Penn applies to her garden, and the laser-sharp focus with which she approaches the business of design and cultivation, this garden (like the gardener) never takes itself too seriously. Planters—some antique and others not precious at all—display succulents

and annuals in surprising combinations of contrasting colors and scale. Here and there a close look reveals ornaments just barely visible amid the sensory swirl of plants around them. Reflecting on her thirty-year adventure, Penn sums it up: "Gardening is very much about taking materials and transforming them in some way. It's the art form one has the least control over, which is also what makes it the most fun." One senses that even with another thirty years to continue her gardening practice, she will be in no danger of ever finishing.

OPPOSITE: Seven-foot tall Scheherazade oriental lilies draw the eye up from this mixed planting of persicaria (foreground), amsonia, bee balm, tropical castor bean, and other annuals and perennials. ABOVE: One of the arrangements that Suzanne Penn creates daily. Dahlias are often the stars, but she experiments with unusual additions, such are various euphorbias and nasturtium leaves. OVERLEAF: A pipevine-draped pergola offers welcome shade from the otherwise sunny garden, while a vintage patio set from the 1940s is the perfect place to relax.

ANCESTORS AND ARCHITECTS

Chestnut Hill

In 1894, when twenty-six-year-old Gertrude Houston married Dr. George Woodward, her father gifted the couple with fifty acres and enough money to build a country estate. It was a fitting wedding present, considering Henry Howard Houston's wealth. Of the many nineteenth-century fortunes amassed in rapidly industrializing Pennsylvania, his came from investments in canals, railroads, oil, and later real estate purchased near where the lines for his Pennsylvania Railroad were to be built.

The newlyweds' property had long been cultivated as farmland carved from the Pennsylvania forest, and, at the time they took ownership, woodland still flanked the banks of the Wissahickon Creek below. The ruins of a nearby nineteenth-century paper mill were visible, along with a Pennsylvania bank barn and low stone walls built by earlier generations of European settlers.

Gertrude and George took the requisite yearlong European honeymoon of their social set and returned in 1895 full of ideas for their new home, which they would name "Krisheim" in a nod to early German inhabitants of the area. The estate would take more than fifteen years to coax into existence, although work on the grounds began early on, with clearing and shaping of the agricultural land into something closer to a private arboretum.

By 1910, the Olmsted Brothers landscape architecture firm was under contract, tasked with creating an Americanized version of an English park that would burnish the grandeur of the Jacobean Revival–style, half-timbered mansion that was then under construction. Plans included a sweeping drive leading to the home, and an extensive series of formal gardens descending behind it. These gardens, which incorporated a summerhouse, pools, fountains, brick-lined terraces supported by massive retaining walls, a wall garden filled with 1,400 varieties of rock garden plants, and a gazebo graced with statuary, took two years to complete.

Neither the Olmsteds nor their clients could have foreseen that the house and gardens, built for the ages, were predicated on a way of life that even for those who could attain it was to be short-lived. The Great Depression, sandwiched between two world wars, eroded the ranks of staff needed to run the estate, and by the 1940s, massive homes requiring mountains of coal for heat had lost their luster in Philadelphia and elsewhere.

The family held on to the property, at least parts of it, longer than many of their peers retained theirs, but by the 1960s, the Gilded Age relic was gifted for use as a religious retreat.

Krisheim's current owner, Chuck Woodward, first became acquainted with the property in 1984, when he was in his early twenties. That year, his grandfather repurchased fifteen acres of the estate from the Presbyterian church and returned it to family ownership. Even after twenty years as an institution, the property was surprisingly intact, if much neglected. Upended flagstones were strewn around the garden. Water features had been filled in, and statues had disappeared. Boxwood hedges were either gap-toothed or overgrown, and no trace remained of the flower beds that had once lined the brick paths. With encouragement and financial backing from his mother and grandmother after his grandfather's death, Chuck (and later his wife, Anna) undertook a landscape restoration that has taken the better part of thirty-five years, culminating with the renovation of the 28,000-square-foot mansion. He started, of course, with the garden.

The Olmsted firm's most famous projects include public spaces like Central Park in New York City and FDR Park in Philadelphia, but it also accepted private commissions, including many on the Main Line and Chestnut Hill neighborhoods in Philadelphia. The iconic Olmsted pastoral landscape calls attention to nature and subordinates decorative elements and details while taking advantage of long views to enhance the spatial perspective. Although Olmsted projects include ample use of built features like walls, bridges, and structures, they are used more to call attention to their surroundings than to themselves. The firm's style was copied widely on many twentieth-century properties, but few authentic Olmsted landscapes survive, and most are only fragments.

With advice from landscape architect Rob Fleming and aided by the original Olmsted plans as well as historic photos taken during the property's glory days, Chuck and Anna Woodward gradually put the gardens back in order. The many dogwoods indicated in the original blueprints were replaced, this time with the newer, pink-flowered cultivars as well as the white-flowered species that were the only type available in the early twentieth century. Missing boxwoods were replaced, conifers were added where they were originally specified, and a grass plot encircled by the drive was reestablished with plantings of low evergreens and perennials as an entrance garden.

Loyalty to the spirits of architects and ancestors notwithstanding, the Woodwards did deviate from the original plans when this made sense. Some plants were no longer available or advisable for use; in other cases, as with the dogwoods, a wider color selection was available, allowing the mostly white garden of the early 1900s to become more colorful. Deer arrived on a summer evening in 1998 and never left, necessitating fencing around the formal gardens and an unappetizing plant palette elsewhere.

PRECEDING OVERLEAF: As part of a decades-long restoration, the long fountain had to be excavated after having been entirely filled in while the property was outside family ownership. It was then enhanced with new plantings.

OPPOSITE: The pastoral quality of the property's parklike setting features specimen trees planted inside a perimeter of mature woodland.

While the garden's "skeleton" was replaced as closely as possible, plenty of spaces between the bones needed to be fleshed out. Double rows of Annabelle hydrangea now line the walkway of an upper terrace, and new perennial beds have been established. The Woodwards, while happy to entertain the idea of change, have also understood that the garden's strongest feature is its architecture, and they are ever vigilant in keeping the plantings from becoming so fussy or blowsy that they detract from the hardscape.

When exploring such a large, complex landscape, one might find it easy to overlook that the garden here was designed for the family's leisure and intended for the contemplation of nature. A meditative quality still permeates the grounds. Mature trees cast dappled shadows, and fallen pine needles soften footsteps. But for the one who manages this vast space, originally maintained by thirty-four full-time gardeners, the time for relaxation and lounging rarely comes. There's just too much to do. Woodward admits that without the family connection, he would never have taken on such a herculean project. But he perseveres, driven by the knowledge that his efforts keep this remnant of his family's history—and of a grand horticultural style now mostly vanished from the region—literally alive.

OPPOSITE: Plantings on the upper terrace are kept relatively simple so as not to compete with the excellent stonework designed by the Olmsted firm and built by master craftsmen a century ago. An espaliered Kousa dogwood softens the massive wall of Wissahickon schist. OVERLEAF: Axial relationships and symmetry are relied upon for the formal areas of the garden, while outside the walls a more naturalistic aesthetic prevails. Here, two approaches to a reflecting pool create a sense of mystery by revealing little of what lies beyond.

ABOVE: A statue of Narcissus perches on the edge of the reflecting pool. This and other original features have been carefully restored and, where needed, returned to their original locations. OPPOSITE: To create perfectly level lawns in the formal gardens the sloping property was terraced into several levels.

PRECEDING OVERLEAF: Low stone walls mark the delineation between the built environment and the stunning backdrop of the Wissahickon Valley. Although intensively designed, the landscape architecture is intentionally subservient to the natural setting.

OPPOSITE: A closeup of the gazebo's stonework. Lush greens of woodland perennials lighten the shady corner: ABOVE: The Annabelle walk, named after the tough, long blooming cultivar of hydrangea that flanks the stone path.

GOD IS IN
THE DETAILS

Rydal

Many styles of American domestic architecture can be associated with straightforward gardening reference points. Think of how bedded-out annuals complement Victorian architecture, boxwoods feature in Colonial revival flower borders, and foundation plantings and perfect front lawns became emblematic of the postwar suburban ranch.

But true mid-century modernism isn't accompanied by such a ready playbook of horticultural options. Many expressions of the style are more notable for a subtractive approach to plants in deference to a primary interest in minimalism and order.

Craig Wakefield had spent years becoming an aficionado of mid-century modernism, even going so far as to retire from dentistry to become a realtor specializing in homes from the era. In 2015, when he came across a 1951 home in Rydal, Pennsylvania, designed by Arthur White, he was thrilled to have found an important instance of early mid-century modernism that he could restore to its glory. With many of the original details intact and others well documented by contemporary photos, the home provided an opportunity for him to dive deep into the movement in which he had long immersed himself. He threw himself into restoring and furnishing the home, seeking sources for the finishes, objects, and furnishings most sympathetic to the house's original look and feel.

But his fealty to the property's origins did not extend to the outdoor space. "I went for the garden I wanted as opposed to having a modern garden," he says without apology. His investigations found no evidence that the three-quarter-acre property ever included a garden. Conversations with the previous owners confirmed his hunch that the landscape—rather than functioning as a focal point—served more as a negative space to frame the home's strong architecture.

Undaunted, Wakefield set to work, applying his meticulous research skills to a learn-as-you-go approach that ultimately resulted in a series of discrete, yet unified outdoor spaces filled with thousands of carefully selected plants and a collection of plein air sculptures. The restrained hand demanded inside the house was allowed a broader and more exuberant expression outdoors. When viewed together, the house and garden seem to engage one another—like two strong personalities whose differing perspectives make for fascinating eavesdropping.

The garden's well-thought-out planning reflects the autodidact's keen desire to understand materials and to synthesize information. But even more important to Wakefield is his goal of creating as much beauty as possible, and for this he relies on his skillful use of color and design to pack each distinct space with interest while also enabling the flow of spaces into one another. The result is a one-of-a-kind garden that feels both personal and universal and that manages to solve problems like stormwater runoff without calling attention to such unromantic topics.

The house is oriented on cardinal points and placed on a diagonal to the property's deeply pitched rectangular lot. The first garden was constructed around a patio outside floor-to-ceiling windows and from its inception was meant to be viewed like a diorama from the indoors. "It was the first place I'd lived that actually had a view of the garden, and so I designed it from the inside," he recalls. A reflecting pool was sited to cast glimmering sunlit reflections deep into the home's interior on the shortest winter days. Today, deep perennial beds feature statuesque thalictrum, bee balm, and rudbeckia specimens that seem to be in conversation with the home's primary-colored exterior wall panels.

A covered walkway leading to the front door from the garage creates a three-sided courtyard enclosing a tiny sea of gravel surrounding planted islands—hostas and Hakone grass near the shady foundation and sedums in the sunnier section.

Although these plants with different light requirements are separated by just a few feet, they are able to thrive because the building's orientation promotes conditions in this garden that range from nearly full shade to all-day sun.

Another early project was any gardener's dream: a sweeping hundred-foot, south-facing boundary line with enough space for a mixed perennial and shrub border staged in front of a curtain of mixed conifers. A combination of faster-growing trees such as cryptomeria created quick privacy, and slower-growing spruces add color and interest. The red foliage of smokebush, weigela, and split-leaf Japanese maples plays off the deeper greens and blues and repeats to unify the long border.

As the gardens unfold, grade changes carved out from the natural contours make the space feel bigger by breaking it into separate areas. While special plants are everywhere, the repetition of strong colors draws attention to the whole picture instead of allowing the eye to rest on just these individuals. Outdoor sculptures, only one allowed per garden area and many of them kinetic, provide sequential focal points. Collected over many years, they include some pieces that Wakefield has designed himself and commissioned from craftspeople and others that have been acquired from well-known artists.

Throughout the property, a long, continuous path leads visitors through a series of spaces— a sloped dry garden banked with boulders, a Japanese-influenced meditation garden, and

PRECEDING OVERLEAF & OPPOSITE: The strict geometry of the house is softened by the presence of ornamental grasses, used frequently throughout the property. The primary colors of the home's paneled sections are repeated throughout the garden, here with blue ageratum and red salvia.

a garden styled after Piet Oudolf's "new perennial" movement, which relies heavily on native ornamental grasses. At the lowest section, a rock-lined swale helps to slow water that pours down from uphill properties during heavy rain, transforming what would become a muddy slick into a (usually) dry creek bed in which shimmering Acorus gramineus, or Japanese sweet flag, plants seem to ripple out from the base of the boulders.

The final addition was created in the middle of the pandemic: an extension of the path to a woodland garden at the bottom of the property. Under mature hardwood trees, the ground is planted with a combination of native shade-loving perennials, as well as hostas and astilbes, for color and interest. At the path's termination, Wakefield—ever attentive to the tiniest feature—created a sculptural "bump" of earth planted

with more acorus plants. Besides being playful, the mound serves as a rotary, directing foot traffic around and back up the path.

Although the garden was established with a plan, both it and the gardener have continued to evolve. Red flowers, initially not part of the color palette, were incorporated after Wakefield noticed how hummingbirds were drawn to them. As for himself, Wakefield allows that he's become more relaxed in the last few years, able to enjoy a slightly wilder-looking garden even if a weed happens to pop up here or there. But a slight loosening of the reins does not mean that this garden is getting out of his control. Instead, the carefully curated and well-tended beds exemplify that the idiom "God is in the details," often attributed to German minimalist architect Ludwig Mies van der Rohe, can be equally applicable to gardens.

OPPOSITE: The slight cantilever of the home is mirrored in the elevated patio. ABOVE: The home's front entrance is connected to the garage by a covered walkway. Colorful, textural beds lined with Corten steel edging manage to be both minimalist and abundant, like much of the garden.

OVERLEAF: The dark purple-brown of the Corten steel sculpture is perfectly matched to the hue of Royal Purple smokebush, itself contrasted by a Colorado blue spruce. Hot-colored perennials and the brown tones of grasses further unify the border.

PRECEDING OVERLEAF LEFT: The garden is designed with sweeps of dramatic color, here with astilbe, persicaria, and grasses. PRECEDING OVERLEAF RIGHT: The flowering stems of dark-leaved Black Lace elderberry. LEFT: To make the sloping site more usable, stone slabs are set into the ground for step risers, banked by large boulders. ABOVE: The garden's density is contrasted with areas of negative space, like this Japanese-inspired gravel garden.

ABOVE: A lichen-covered boulder cleaved and set with a stone slab becomes a bench that's effective as a focal point as well as a place to relax. LEFT: The bright red flowers of bee balm are used frequently in the garden and attract hummingbirds. OPPOSITE TOP: A reflecting pool is only inches deep but reflects shimmering light into the home through a wall of windows. OPPOSITE BELOW: Beautiful but also utilitarian, dry laid stones create a safe passage to the lower area of the steeply inclined property.

THE NATURE
OF TIME

Chestnut Hill

Some aesthetic experiences can be appreciated in a single moment (a painting, for example, or the photographs on these pages). But others are enjoyed as they unfold over time (music, literature, dance). Most gardens belong in the second category, and few exemplify this temporal quality more than that created by James and Anne-Marie Corner in the Chestnut Hill neighborhood of Philadelphia. Here, the harmonics between nature and design generate an ongoing series of experiences that are never exactly repeated or copied.

In 2012, the Corners, longtime residents of the area, were surprised to find that the open field they regularly passed on their neighborhood walks also had a house on it, and that both the land and the building were for sale. The home, a renovated, early-nineteenth-century barn, had originally been part of the adjacent Woodward family property, Krisheim (see page 79). The house was too small for their needs, but the four-acre property was magical—a sunny hillside that descended to a wet area adjacent to the Wissahickon Valley Park. They took the plunge, knowing it would take years of work to adapt the house and the grounds to their vision.

Surrounded by woods, the land had been kept open since its earlier agricultural applications, first as pasture and later as an orchard. Annual mowing had prevented the woods from encroaching, but invasive species had crept in, intermingling with the overgrown pasture grass. The property was too big to garden in any conventional way and most of it was too steep to allow large swaths of lawn had that been desired (it wasn't). For his own garden, James, a landscape architect with prominent public projects all over the world, embraced a philosophy of letting nature lead, allowing the land to reveal itself rather than imposing a highly designed intervention upon it.

A closer inspection of the marshy area at the low point of the property led to the discovery that it was actually a series of man-made, spring-fed ponds that had silted up over the decades. The Corners brought in heavy equipment to dredge the ponds and take away the silt; they followed that with more work to liberate the ponds' stone retaining walls of vines and weeds. Once cleared, the ponds refilled with fresh water and immediately began to attract wildlife—an element that would be important to the next phase of the project.

The Corners decided that a meadow could be not only a practical and beautiful approach for their landscape but also a haven for wildlife. They worked with landscape designer Larry Weaner, a specialist with decades of experience in meadow methodology, to come up with a plan. Weaner knew the biggest challenge in establishing a successful meadow here would be managing weeds. Fortunately, most of the property was sunny and dry, with not particularly fertile soil—conditions that many native meadow plants can tolerate but that many weeds cannot. The trick would be to get the new plants growing so densely that they would smother competing weed seeds already in the soil.

The existing vegetation was primarily overgrown nonnative turf or pasture grass, possibly descended from when the property was used for grazing in past centuries. Here and there, naturally occurring clumps of native broomsedge had also taken hold and were thriving. Weaner's tactic was to retain the native grass while eradicating the European grass, which was ecologically incompatible with a meadow planting. He applied an early-spring application of herbicide to hit the cool-season European grass just as it began growing and before the warm-season native grass broke dormancy. The resulting open areas were seeded with a mix of native meadow grasses and wildflowers, along with an annual grass to stabilize the soil and prevent weed seeds from taking hold. The area was mowed once a month the first

season after it was planted, knocking back the height of the annual grass and letting light reach the seedlings. Once the seedlings were established, larger nursery-grown plants were added in the fall. The meadow took three years to fill in. Weaner is quick to point out, however, that no meadow can ever be considered "mature," as the plant makeup is constantly adapting to the conditions of the site.

Weaner developed a number of specific plant combinations that were ecologically appropriate for each area of the property. The most aggressive natives were placed around the perimeter, where they would face the most weed pressure from the surrounding woods. Other mixes were chosen for the main, sunny meadow area and another sloping area that receives more shade. Path edges and areas near the house were planted with more intricate, smaller plant combinations to lend a gardenesque effect and act as a mid-layer between the taller meadow and the lawn.

Successful meadows need to be interesting in every season, and not just for aesthetic reasons. Having plants constantly in bloom or fruiting maximizes the amount of wildlife that can be supported throughout the year. Anne-Marie has become a serious birder, and the increasingly biodiverse meadow attracts a wide range of avian species, including many songbirds that prefer open spaces. A path encircling the meadow both prevents weeds from encroaching and allows the Corners to engage with the farther reaches of

PRECEDING OVERLEAF: The Corners enlarged the home (which was originally a barn) and added windows to create a greater connection with the landscape.

OPPOSITE: Swaths of naturalistic plantings, here lavender and amsonia, extend almost to the swimming pool's edge.

PRECEDING OVERLEAF: The only patch of lawn on the property is on the relatively flat area adjacent to the home. Steep terrain and a desire to provide habitat informed the decision to plant the rest of the property as a meadow. ABOVE: Old piers built of native stone anchor a seating area at the bottom of the property. LEFT: The passage of time is apparent in the twisted stem of an old sassafras tree, scarred by the years but still vital. OPPOSITE TOP: Steps are cut into the grade to permit easier passage through the landscape. OPPOSITE BELOW: Yew trees, gnarled with age and the effects of deer browse, flank steps leading down to the Wissahickon Valley.

the property. They estimate that they've boosted biodiversity from probably a few dozen species, many of them invasive, to hundreds of different types of plants and animals all working together in a natural way. "Just in a beautiful, poetic existence, really," notes James.

The work of James's firm, James Corner Field Operations, can be found around the world, but its most well-known project in the United States is the High Line, a twenty-two-block linear park built on a disused elevated train trestle on Manhattan's West Side. At first there seems to be no comparison between the firm's signature public project and this home garden, yet these two very different spaces share a sensibility beyond an emphasis on native plants. Like the High Line, the meadow can only be experienced by moving through it, allowing the visitor to gradually view features that have been intentionally blocked by tall grasses or framed narrowly so they emerge only upon close approach.

Of all the compelling qualities of this landscape, perhaps the most evocative is the sense of time itself. The meadow, open to the sky, changes in appearance depending on the time of day and the angle of the sun. More dramatic are the transformations that take place throughout the seasons. Springtime is about the flowering trees at the woodland's edges, which the Corners thickened with additions of redbuds, dogwoods, cherries, and magnolias. Summer showcases the big meadow blooming amid the cacophony of insects in the still humidity. In autumn, the misty meadow goes from green to gold, while the trees turn shades of yellow, russet, red, and orange. In winter, the hues shift from gold to orange-brown, and the softness of the meadow plants generate drama against the skeletal tree trunks and branches.

While certain annual changes in the landscape are somewhat expected (though never entirely the same), other variations come as a surprise as ecological processes evolve over time. Some plants may not make themselves known until ten years after they've been planted, while others dominate in the early years before being superseded by others. In the Corners' meadow, a large sweep of pink muhly grass has receded and been replaced by broomsedge. Luckily, the gardeners are partial to both.

And happily, they realize that the more time they spend in their meadow, the more deeply they become attached—to the plants, the wildlife, and the hourly, daily, and seasonal changes that will continue to be led by the forces of nature.

PRECEDING OVERLEAF: Sight lines have been carefully considered to preserve the view of the pond, which is the destination of several of the property's pathways.

OPPOSITE: A view up into the meadow. The plantings are brought right up to the pathways, allowing close observation of the many living species that now are drawn to the landscape.

OPPOSITE: The meadow as an ever-changing tapestry of color, form, and texture. No hour, day, month, or year is ever the same. THIS PAGE: 1. The fruit of an umbrella magnolia. 2. Mist often settles in the bowl-shaped landscape. 3. Ruby-crowned kinglet. 4. Insects that like open areas, such as this skipper, are drawn to the meadow. 5. Frogs and other amphibians have returned to the ponds. 6. Yellowthroat, a native songbird. 7. A tiger swallowtail alights on perennial mountain mint. 8. Many species of native insects provide pollination and food for wildlife.

A PEACEABLE KINGDOM

Frenchtown

Those who garden understand innately what a balm the pursuit offers to body and soul—purging the spirit of burdens both big and small. This intention has found its expression on 110 acres of mellow, purplish-hued soil near the Delaware River. Although extensive in acreage, the cultivated landscape reveals itself only at the end of a gently curving quarter-mile drive lined with thousands of daffodils and red buckeye trees. At that point, the view unveils a rambling farmhouse situated in a magical setting. The home's Federal-style front façade, with a historic core enlarged by nineteenth- and twentieth-century additions, is set off to advantage by a series of low, brick-lined parterres containing simple but elegant plantings anchored by mature river birches. As in many surviving eighteenth-century farmhouses, its oldest section is three rooms high by one room wide, but unlike most similar houses of its time, this structure's surroundings have retained their original rural character, with neither a highway nor gas station within earshot or eyesight.

Only in the back of the gracious home is the greater part of the landscape visible in a breathtaking wide expanse of field, pasture, garden, water, and forest. Most of the property is contained within a shallow, contoured bowl, as if the landscape is cupped in the hand of a gentle giant. At the lowest point, six ponds (one with the tiniest possible private island) are connected by bridges and fed by a waterfall, and naturalistic swaths of perennials and shrubs adorn the gently sloping banks.

The landscape's feeling of going back in time isn't accidental. The design was directly inspired by eighteenth-century English landscape architect Capability Brown, whose work the owner was introduced to on her many visits to English gardens. Brown, rather than implementing the formal style of garden design dominant at that time, used a more naturalistic approach that often included damming a stream to create a picturesque succession of ponds and interspersing pastoral belts and copses of trees in the otherwise open country house landscapes on which he worked. Both of those strategies have been incorporated here. In another nod to Brown, a modern interpretation on a classical Roman temple is a focal point when viewed from the house and is also the site for family musical and dance performances.

Although she has a background in design, the property's owner has practiced law for most of her career, and the lushly soft environs lend a

welcome reprieve from the hard-charging, adversarial daily life of a litigator whose average case can take ten years to resolve. The landscape seems to deeply exhale not just oxygen, but billowing clouds of tall perennials and waving field grasses, which are shadowed by the irregular forms of mature hardwood trees with limbs that have ample room to extend over the open land. The ambient soundtrack is a playlist provided by the call of songbirds in the woods and fields. Closer to the house, the back garden is more formal, but it contains few hard edges, walls, or impenetrable barriers; this is not a garden of discrete rooms in which secrets or surprises lurk.

Adding to the good karma of the property is a temporal sanctuary: an extensive collection of ducks, swans, chickens, and rescue animals, including cows, horses (full-size and miniature), and several types of goats. The undomesticated range of the menagerie is represented by a self-sufficient pride of peafowl that roost in the rafters of an equipment shed, showing majestic disdain for whoever alights on the tractor underneath them. As the peafowl are uncontained and unwilling to respect property lines, over time most of the neighbors also host peafowl.

While the owner has lived here since the 1980s, her development of the landscape has been a more recent pursuit. Early attempts were challenged by the sheer size of the property. The common and often-effective technique of sectioning a garden into different "rooms" or zones didn't appeal, as the goal was to keep the space unified and to preserve the views of the panoramic landscape. A good friend was enlisted to help, landscape designer Renny Reynolds, who had mastered large-scale garden design on his well-known Hortulus Farm. Drawing on his earlier career as an event planner, Reynolds intuitively understood how the placement of certain elements could make a space feel either larger or smaller and impart a dramatic sense of proportion and scale. The most theatrical design element he used on this property is also the most subtle; the sinuous lines of the ponds are echoed by extensive waves of plants such as packeras, amsonias, and stachys, which ripple outward and up the gradual banks and unify the entire landscape.

The property design has been underway for less than ten years, though the result feels like the consequence of centuries of cultivation. But as with all gardens, this one is always evolving. In the aftermath of extreme weather and emerging pathogens, more than two thousand trees have been removed for replacement with the hardiest of native varieties. An ongoing project to clear the woods of invasive vines to make riding trails seems downright Sisyphean. While the demands of managing a property of this size and complexity would be daunting for many, for the owner the pull is too powerful to consider any other kind of life. "I love to travel," she muses, "but honestly, I'd be perfectly happy never to leave here."

PRECEDING OVERLEAF: In the farmyard, the pale red color of red buckeye flowers is repeated in the antique door pediment repurposed as a support for wisteria.

OPPOSITE: The serenity of the landscape is particularly felt in the early morning light.

PRECEDING OVERLEAF: A spring-fed waterfall fills the ponds. OPPOSITE: If this cow seems particularly content, it should be. No trouble is spared to give the farm's animals the best possible life. ABOVE: Domestic fowl under the cover of a magnificent Chinese wisteria in full bloom. At one point, this peaceable kingdom of birds and animals numbered two hundred, but altogether the various species are now down to around 125. OVERLEAF: Although naturalistic in appearance, all the plants have been chosen carefully to bring season-long interest to the garden.

OPPOSITE: The soft colors of early spring light up the landscape. THIS PAGE: 1. A few of the farm's larger residents. 2. Swans patrol the pond. 3. A modern kinetic sculpture adds another dimension to the grounds. 4. A male peacock. Many roost in the barn beyond, as well as on the neighboring properties. 5. A decorative urn as a focal point on the back patio. 6. Just two of the peaceable kingdom's inhabitants. OVERLEAF: Long drifts of spring-blooming yellow packera emphasize the sinuous curves of the little creek running through the property.

THE PHILADELPHIA STORY

Bryn Mawr

The first generation of Main Line Philadelphia estates were nineteenth-century showplaces for those who had made fortunes in coal, beer, or textiles, and which quickly became obsolete, the few survivors existing as convents or private schools. But the early twentieth century brought another building wave—this time for people more likely to be investment bankers, stockbrokers, or lawyers. Many of their large, well-constructed properties remain very livable by today's standards, their enduring elegance exuding a second-generation confidence of perhaps having less to prove. Leslie Miller and Richard Worley's property in Bryn Mawr is a product of this era and hews closely to its tradition while reflecting a strong concern for the environment and their own interests as gardeners and collectors.

Miller and Worley have long collected art and antiques, mainly from Philadelphia and the Delaware Valley. Their discerning eye is as evident outdoors as it is inside. They have clearly mastered (and enjoy) the subtlety between what makes one thing "good" and another "better." Similar to the style of the antique-filled rooms of the home, the garden's first impression on a visitor is that it's beautiful yet livable, tasteful, and very well maintained. After spending time in the house and garden, one begins to realize that the couple have taken collecting (whether plants or objects) to a remarkable level of connoisseurship, where no one element screams for attention but every single component is of excellent form and quality. "Just as is the case with collecting art and antiques, cultivating our garden has been a long-term journey for us," remarks Miller. "In neither case did we have a vision of the destination."

Their story began with the 1985 purchase of their home, designed by one of the Main Line's most preeminent builders, Walter K. Durham, just before the social, economic, and cultural shifts of World War II. They had looked at enough houses to know that they loved Durham's architecture—well-sited homes made of native stone on attractive properties. This particular home was in the French country style, not exactly their taste, and the original three acres had been subdivided with a somewhat incongruous modern home erected on its lower section, compromising the view and privacy. But there was enough to commend the property to outweigh their reservations, and they committed to becoming its next stewards.

Although Miller grew up around horticulture (her mother, now in her nineties, is still adding to a private arboretum she's created in the Pennsylvania countryside, and her grandmother was also a gardener), she never had a garden of her own. The Bryn Mawr property at one time featured a boxwood maze and intricate perennial beds, but the only traces left when she and Worley took ownership were some venerable trees of great character. She began her journey with very little of an existing garden and minimal understanding of how to go about cultivating one, but she cared deeply about preserving the property's legacy and was eager to educate herself.

Visits to the Philadelphia Flower Show, consultations with garden designers, and tours of private and public gardens ensued. Miller is quick to credit the horticultural professionals who have worked alongside her, some for decades, to gradually build a living collection of plants that are exceptional not always because they are rare varieties, but because they are maintained in a constant state of near aesthetic and cultural perfection.

Over the years, the couple has had hardscape installed, perennial beds added, low walls built, and a pond dug by an old cherry tree. Each introduction brought into sharper focus Miller's vision: a balanced garden with clean lines featuring a variety of plants that work together but also connect with the larger landscape. "There's now a wonderfully firm foundation, but the garden itself is constantly changing," she says. As examples, she points to a tree that was moved a few feet to make room for a new bed, a row of shrubs that were to be dug up and replanted elsewhere on the property, and a rock garden about to undergo major design changes.

With the opportunity to purchase back the subdivided lot in the early 2010s, Miller and Worley were able to restore the property's original footprint and increase the size of the garden. In short order, the anachronistic modern house was demolished, and a walled garden was created in its place. Several long, terraced stone walls, an extensive compost system, and cold frames were also added to make the sloped property more usable. With the extra space, Miller expanded her assortment of special trees and increased the varieties of hostas, hydrangeas, and hellebores she grows. She also introduced dozens of peonies, roses, and dahlias that are used in arrangements throughout the house.

Unusual shrubs like daphniphyllums are deftly intermixed with classic landscape anchors like hollies, rhododendrons, and boxwoods, and all are exquisitely pruned and perfectly cultivated. Dwarf conifers and unusual Japanese maples in the rock garden are groomed to bonsai standards, and elsewhere naturalistic thickets of woody plants are juxtaposed with perfectly clipped spheres and cones. Three sides of the property are bordered by towering hedges of mixed conifers, the perfect backdrop for sweetgum, magnolia, and dogwood specimens and a grove of ornamental cherries.

PRECEDING OVERLEAF: The long perennial border is the focal point of the back garden. Here, the soft tones of artemesias, sedums, and pale blue agastaches play well against the blue-green shutters and trim of the home. In recent years Miller has incorporated a larger percentage of native perennials to increase benefits to wildlife. OPPOSITE: A perfectly espaliered pear tree.

PRECEDING OVERLEAF: The garden often juxtaposes natural and manicured forms, such as these pruned boxwoods growing under spring-flowering trees.

ABOVE: The couple designed the low wall to provide the ideal backdrop for their collection of garden antiques.

Indoor plants are also a passion. Not surprisingly, Miller's impeccable specimens have won multiple ribbons at the Philadelphia Flower Show. A lot of these plants spend summers outdoors on specially built benches, overwintering in a modest-size greenhouse beyond the garage and a larger one off-site. Indoors or out, care for these plants never stops. Throughout the year, specimens of pelargoniums, orchids, succulents, tropicals, topiaries, and other potted plants are continually plucked, tweezed, twirled, and wired to perfection.

Miller's lifetime love for animals is evidenced by the oversized French bloodhound garden sculpture, which seems to stand guard over the landscape; the many birdbaths and bird feeders scattered around the property; and the continual addition of native plants in the perennial beds. By incorporating native milkweed, goldenrod, echinacea, and aster plants, she says, the garden now attracts increased numbers of hummingbirds and butterflies. Simultaneously, the looser forms and varying heights of these plants have actually enhanced the appeal of the undulating border.

A few vestiges of the era in which this garden was originally established remain. Here and there, trees like a weeping Norway spruce and a gnarled flowering cherry—both the height of horticultural fashion a hundred years ago—are preserved, and the remnants of a grand beech allée still stand sentry at the property's entrance.

Miller and Worley have spent decades developing their garden, endeavoring to make it ever more beautiful and livable while creating a place that reflects their own interests and aesthetics. Yet they have also managed to preserve the character of this living connection to an earlier era of American gardening, in which landscapes were more often considered integral to a home, and as such were allocated the energy and resources needed to reach their maximum beauty. After spending an afternoon here, the idea of committing extraordinary care on gardens and plants doesn't seem like an unreasonable pursuit or a practice relegated to a bygone era. In this garden, the relationship between past and present, so fragile in most landscapes, is still very much alive.

148

OPPOSITE: A majestic weeping Norway spruce relic from this garden's first golden era in the 1940s. THIS PAGE: 1. One of the many antique garden statues. 2. The tropical lavender star flower is overwintered indoors. 3. The speckled stem of Amorphophallis, otherwise known as corpse flower for the foul smell of its blossoms. 4. Native redbud in bud. 5. A cluster of airplants, which in nature attach themselves to tree branches. 6. A delightful mixed container of low-maintenance tender succulents 7. Although Miller is an animal lover, these life-size deer are perhaps the only ones that are welcome in the garden. 8. The king of the jungle presiding over his subjects.

ABOVE: Peony shoots emerge red at the same time as Siberian squill begins to bloom. OPPOSITE: A rock garden with many specimens of pendulous conifer and deciduous trees wraps around one corner of the house. OVERLEAF: The garden's strong structure is particularly visible in winter, when the bare coral branches of Sango Kaku Japanese maple stand out in the landscape.

COMMON GROUND

Mount Airy

The two practices on which Syd Carpenter has focused much of her adult life—creating art and designing gardens—are related expressions for a visual communicator. As a sculptor working primarily in ceramics, she concentrates on making art (and for many years teaching art as a professor at Swarthmore College) during the colder months. In the warmer seasons, she devotes her time to gardening.

For decades, the essential thread she has explored in her art and horticulture vocations is the meaning of land and how soil—a substance that is the source of all life, sustenance, and beauty—also represents a painful darkness. Conflicts over land have been waged since the beginning of humankind. In crucial ways, they have shaped and stained the trajectory of American history, beginning when indigenous tribes were forced off their land by European settlers and continuing with the practice of enslavement that forced millions of African Americans to toil without pay on land they could never call their own.

And yet land—the agent of so much suffering and conflict—also has incredible regenerative power to heal itself and repair connections between people. Whether that land is an expanse of pristine nature, a working farm, a community garden, or an urban backyard, it can be an instrument of reconciliation and a place to literally and figuratively find common ground. In Carpenter's view, a cup of potting soil holding a cutting is made of land, as are her own clay sculptures. And her approach to cultivating her own property is in alignment with her belief that gardening can help people connect with one another and become more respectful and appreciative of the earth, and also help heal the damage incurred by past wrongs. "I think that gardeners can play an important part in mending some of the ripping and tearing of our society and our planet," she explains.

A Philadelphian since childhood, she credits her grandmother Indiana Hutson's roots in the rural South with her own eventual embrace of gardening. Hutson was part of a huge demographic shift in the first half of the twentieth century, when millions of black Americans migrated north, leaving behind agricultural work in the Jim Crow-era South to pursue economic opportunities created by the burgeoning manufacturing industry in cities like Philadelphia. With many of the migrants came a deep knowledge of gardening. A victory garden helped feed Hutson's seven children, and

Carpenter's mother, Ernestine, grew up gardening alongside her mother. As a child, Carpenter was aware of the importance of gardening to her family. But her own interest wasn't awakened until she became a homeowner and began thinking about the intersection of gardening with her own personal and cultural history.

Carpenter's garden sits on an appealing corner of a leafy block in the Northwest Philadelphia neighborhood of Mount Airy, across from a public elementary school and on a street whose sidewalks see many passersby throughout the day. For a city property, it feels surprisingly inviting; indeed, the entrance gate has been removed to allow a peek into a petite yet complete world she and her husband, Steve Donegan (also an artist), have established over the last thirty years. Here plants and objects are used as artistic media, placed intentionally with consideration of their colors, forms, and contrasts to engender a whole and satisfying aesthetic experience. As an artist, she is always thinking about the viewer and will rework an area if she senses the eye will move past it too quickly. A recent example was replacing a mixed planting of tall flowering annuals in a large container with a simple mass planting of irises to provide a better contrast to the exuberant mixed border behind it and give the eye a place to settle on in this otherwise busy scene.

Mature trees provide areas of restful shade, but in other areas, sunlight beams down on colorful flowerbeds. Perennials with dramatic foliage act as counterpoints for the many other textures throughout the garden, and every focal point is balanced between a main element (whether a plant or an object) and living and nonliving components that complete the picture. Carpenter sees gardening as a collaborative process between the gardener and nature, with the gardener trying to anticipate how a plant will behave (and attempting to orchestrate how it will relate to the other players) while remaining open to the likelihood that what nature actually has in store will be unexpected. The idea of a controlled garden that adheres to strict parameters and doesn't constantly evolve is not one that interests her; as she puts it, "Plants must be allowed to digress."

The only plant noticeably absent from Carpenter's garden is lawn grass. Instead of turf to walk on, pathways made variously of brick, gravel, or stone pavers wend their way through the landscape, guiding visitors to water features, seating areas, and viewing spots where they can stop and admire a mixed border swollen with seasonally attuned plantings that boast blooms in a staggered progression for most of the year. Although plants are the stars of the show, nonliving objects placed at every juncture and in each viewshed play important supporting roles. Some of these are pieces of art, while others are repurposed architectural or industrial objects possessing intricate shapes that relate to the complex forms of the ornamental plants that intermingle with them.

PRECEDING OVERLEAF: The contorted branches of a weeping redbud echo the round forms of the found and made objects hung for display on a brick wall.

OPPOSITE: Carpenter's clay wall sculpture with pots of hardy variegated English ivy adds interest to a stucco wall.

OPPOSITE: A view of the sidewalk. An ancient deutzia with interesting bark long predates the current garden. The corner property is intensively gardened along the street as a way to engage neighbors in the pleasures of gardening. ABOVE: The slope functions as an overflow area for extra plants, here yellow corydalis, a caramel-colored heuchera, maidenhair fern, campanula, and a brightly hued mophead hydrangea.

With limited square footage in her yard, Carpenter is constantly looking for ways to maximize the space that can be gardened. Eight inches of soil spread over unused bulkhead doors leading to the basement have become a new planting area—more land. While the soil is shallow, it manages to support a collection of perfectly happy ferns and hostas. She has even extended her garden to vertical planes, growing vines up structures and walls and crafting a clay wall sculpture that supports terra-cotta pots planted with variegated ivy.

Over the years, her gardening footprint has gradually expanded from the heart of the property to the margins, where banks sloping down to the sidewalk are filled with a mix of sun- and shade-loving annuals, perennials, shrubs, and groundcovers. The display begins in early spring with masses of bulbs and ends with the last fall-flowering plants. Originally used as an overflow area for plants she couldn't squeeze in elsewhere, it has over the decades evolved into a spectacular stand-alone garden, well-known among friends and even strangers. It's also Carpenter's gift to the neighborhood, as its siting makes it visible only from the street, not from the house. Now a beloved feature in the community, this perimeter garden, perhaps more than any other part of the property, represents the clearest expression of Carpenter's gardening philosophy. Here on exhibit is her talent for facilitating dialogue between people and gardens and for creating a sense of place and belonging for anyone who can appreciate the splendor that is conjured from the soil.

LEFT: The private backyard is screened by evergreens and is home to a collection of plants for shade, including many varieties of hostas and ferns. Found, made, and repurposed objects are placed throughout the garden.

LEFT: In the sunniest part of the garden, hot colored flowering plants like this orange geum contrast with the dark foliage of a weeping Forest Pansy redbud. ABOVE: The ephemeral spring-blooming bleeding heart peeks through a large-leafed hosta.

OPPOSITE: Chocolate lace flower, a reseeding annual. THIS PAGE: 1. Donegan's delicate metal hanging planters 2. A metal screen, also made by Donegan. 3. Korean bellflower. 4. One of Carpenter's nature-inspired clay vessels. 5. An industrial object given new life as a garden ornament. 6. Rodgersia stems repeat the hues of couple's artwork 7. A climbing hydrangea vine clings to a carved wooden pillar.

A PAST WITH A PEDIGREE

Chestnut Hill

One of the few pieces of private land anywhere near Philadelphia that has been continuously farmed since the 1680s, Erdenheim Farm is a large property with a fascinating history. Records show it was first purchased from the Lenni Lenape as part of a larger land transaction in exchange for kettles, guns, shoes, tobacco, and other quotidian items.

Its many iterations have included eras in which the name Erdenheim was known throughout the country for the thoroughbred horses that were bred and raised here and for the famous people who called the property home. But in quieter times, the farm saw only modest activity, shrinking as sections were sold and most animals were dispersed. As centuries passed the world dramatically changed around the farm, making its future existence increasingly uncertain. Each time it changed ownership, the neighboring communities of Flourtown and Chestnut Hill would speculate anxiously about its fate. No one wanted to see the beloved farm—one of the most recognizable private estates in the region—disappear as so many others of its kind had. Yet the attributes that made the farm so special—475 acres of pastoral landscape dotted with dozens of antique buildings and plentiful sheep and cows grazing on either side of the Wissahickon Creek—were more representative of an eighteenth- or nineteenth-century country gentleman's ideal than that of a typical endeavor undertaken today.

The current owners, Peter and Bonnie McCausland, purchased Erdenheim Farm in 2009 and completely embrace the commitment that such a property requires. Their tenure follows a series of eminent owners, once Erdenheim became recognized in the mid-nineteenth century as the farm that raised unbeatable racehorses. Sited above a seam of limestone, the farm boasts more alkaline soil than is found anywhere nearby and is ideal for growing the grass and grain that horses thrive upon. Indeed, the name of the nearest municipality—Flourtown—points to Erdenheim Farm's early significance as a grain producer.

The farm's best-known era began in the early 1900s, when the fabulously wealthy Widener family became associated with the property. Having made a fortune in street railway companies, they were leaders in the Gilded Age society. After the patriarch and his eldest son perished on the *Titanic*, the fortune was left to the remaining younger son, George D. Widener Jr. While still

in his twenties, he acquired Erdenheim Farm and set about making changes that would put his property on par with the greatest estates of Philadelphia; Newport, Rhode Island; and Manhattan's Fifth Avenue.

Widener, a serious horse breeder and gentleman farmer, removed many of the nineteenth-century farm structures. He then commissioned society architect Horace Trumbauer to design bespoke equestrian facilities, barnyards, stables, and other outbuildings for sheep and cows—partly English Cotswolds, partly Norman style. Trumbauer also made extensive alterations to an early-nineteenth-century farmhouse with an awkward later-nineteenth-century addition, transforming the anachronistic structure into a dignified, six-columned, Georgian-style country house.

Significant changes were also made to the landscape. Although the prevailing pastoral aesthetic was carefully preserved, the most prominent landscape architects of the time were engaged to bring modern elegance to the old farm. Jacques Gréber, most renowned for his work designing the Champs-Élysées–inspired Benjamin Franklin Parkway in Philadelphia, was hired to create a large, formal walled garden overlooked by a great glass conservatory. Horace Trumbauer added the pièce de résistance, a fountain-fed cascade rill that empties into a pool at the bottom of the garden.

The Widener family presided over Erdenheim Farm until the death of Fitz Eugene Dixon Jr., the nephew of George D. Widener Jr., in 2006. An unsettled period ensued, with parties representing the interests of developers and preservationists each working to secure pieces of the property, a situation eventually resolved by the McCauslands' decision to purchase and inhabit the farm and preserve it in perpetuity. Several years of pressing business interests then demanded their attention, and only when they turned their full focus to the property, did the magnitude of their undertaking become clear. While the gentleman's farm had been fairly well maintained, it had lost its crisp definition. Buildings and fences needed restoration, as did the gardens, which had become progressively less interesting and varied as plants became overgrown or died and were not replaced. And the McCauslands had their own ideas of what it would take to make the property feel like theirs.

Over ten years later, Erdenheim Farm is as alive with activity as it has ever been. More than 500 sheep, cattle, goats, and chickens live here, many rare breeds among them. After an absence of many years, thoroughbred horses again inhabit the historic stables. A large meadow was added to the landscape to serve as a riparian buffer for the creek. A commercial-grade composting system processes all the farm's organic material, while a one-acre vegetable garden supplies a weekly farm stand.

As for the ornamental gardens, they are back to being wholly and beautifully planted. Although the McCauslands accede that their personal style gravitates toward a more subtle aesthetic, the period restoration was carried out faithfully with full

PRECEDING OVERLEAF: Sheep in the meadow in front of the restored Norman-style sheep barn.

OPPOSITE: A magnificent elm tree stands sentinel next to the home, with the orchard in the foreground just coming into bloom.

respect for the property's historical significance. The formal garden, which still retained 100-year-old specimens of irises and peonies, was restored using the Olmsted Brothers' and Gréber's and Trumbauer's original plans as reference. Today, the crevices of the magnificent cascade rill's stone walls are embellished by classic rock-garden plants like irises and catmint, and water once again flows down the length of the garden into a crystal-clear pond. On the level above the garden, dogwoods planted in a row stand guard.

The vista garden, designed by the Olmsteds to offer a perfect sight line to the house, was equally in need of renovation. Parts of a long grass walk flanked by classic shrubs such as spireas, azaleas, viburnums, and yews against a backdrop of mature hardwoods and conifers were looking a bit gap-toothed and had also been overtaken with vines and weeds. Gradually, with additions of herbaceous plants like ferns, amsonias, and golden groundsel, this historic garden has been reclaimed.

The McCauslands felt freer to express their own tastes more fully around the house, which is situated on a rise with magnificent pastoral views that no garden could possibly outcompete. Instead, they focused on making beds that are best experienced as the winding drive approaches a rectangular motor court. Garden designer Nina Schneider helped them design a sweeping shrub and perennial garden accented by the columnar hornbeam trees. Underneath, undulating swaths of peonies, purple irises, lady's mantles, and salvias flank a wide, curving grass path. The garden is an effective foil to the formal geometric symmetry of the classical Georgian home, which becomes visible partway up the drive. By coincidence—or perhaps as evidence that all good designers think alike—the homeowners later discovered a long-lost Gréber plan for a similar garden that had never been executed.

All of the first-floor windows of the home are French doors, and they, along with several patios, seating areas, and a long, columned porch, allow for the enjoyment of uninterrupted views of the landscape. From a loggia garden outside a conservatory attached to the house, the McCauslands can witness the blanket of white fog that sometimes settles over the creek valley and that early on gave the township its name, Whitemarsh.

Despite the refined domestic architecture, the agricultural functions of Erdenheim Farm are never screened from sight or in any way downplayed. "One of the things we love is that the property goes from formal to agricultural to naturalistic very quickly," remarks Peter McCausland. Ornate wrought-iron gates, created by Samuel Yellin, quickly give way to split-rail farm fences. A productive peach and apple orchard, created by the McCauslands, is laid out in a grid just below the house, while a bit further off, sheepdogs keep watch over the herd. Says Bonnie: "We never forget that we live on a farm."

OPPOSITE: 1. One of the rare Arapawa goats raised on the farm. There are fewer than 500 of this ancient species worldwide. 2. Harvesting microgreens. 3. In spring, lambs must be fed every four hours, day and night. 4. The race stable was designed by Horace Trumbauer and is one of only a few of its kind. OVERLEAF: Fireflies in the meadow on a summer night.

ABOVE: One of the farm's Highland cattle.
RIGHT: While there are a number of staff
and rental homes on the property, its scale
is such that most views are unbroken by
more than a glimpse of architecture. Long
views of fields with trees in the distance
make it hard to believe the property is
adjacent to a major city. OVERLEAF: A
meadow of annual wildflowers regularly
stops traffic, and a wisp of mist that gave
the township the name Whitemarsh is
visible in the air.

PRECEDING OVERLEAF: Along with a series of sweeping drives, the Olmsted firm designed this five-arch stone bridge spanning the Wissahickon. RIGHT: The Georgian style of the home is formal, but the surroundings quickly transition back to the pastoral. Wrought-iron gates by Samuel Yellin separate the courtyard from the garden.

LEFT: One of the few cascading rills in the US harkens back to another era, as does the glass conservatory at the top of the incline. The formal garden contained hundreds of feet of perennial borders laid out in a design by the Olmsted Brothers firm. ABOVE: An antique stone urn atop a pedestal. OVERLEAF: Tidy rows of peach trees on the slope below the house are both productive and beautiful.

187

PAST PERFECT

Swarthmore

Charles Cresson remembers how his nearly lifelong relationship with horticulture began. In seventh grade, his grandmother gave him a book about bonsai, the then-obscure Japanese art of training and dwarfing woody plants. His was a clannish family; in the 1880s, his great-grandfather had purchased twenty acres of "Hedgleigh," a working farm in Swarthmore, Delaware County, and developed the land into an attractive suburban community. By the 1960s, some of his descendants were still living within the same few blocks, and Cresson was growing up in the house his grandfather had built in 1911, a solid, two-story center hall Colonial.

Today, he remains in that house and continues to carefully tend the bonsai collection he started as a middle schooler after reading and rereading the slim volume from his grandmother (a book that stays on his shelf). For Cresson, the practice of gardening is much more than a hobby or even a profession. It inexorably ties him to his family members and their history. In conversation, he often uses the plural pronoun "we" when discussing the garden: "We lost two big pines here," he'll say. Since he's the only person in residence, one at first wonders who is included in

"we." But then it becomes evident that although he has no children of his own, he is constantly aware of his role as steward of this property his ancestors have owned for more than one hundred years and hoped to keep in the family for future generations.

A visitor's first impression is that the Cresson garden contains a lot of detail and a lot of plants. Like most collectors, he's reluctant to devote space to multiples of any one kind of plant when that real estate could be given over to numerous different species and cultivars. Instead of featuring a row of the same variety of hydrangea, for example, his property contains various garden-worthy specimens in that genus, with one or two examples of each type placed throughout the landscape. What keeps the garden from feeling chaotic or disorganized is a strong yet simple framework, meticulous attention to detail (even the lawn is hand-weeded), and a focus on the interplay between one plant and its neighbors, which promotes a sense of cohesion.

The last time Cresson tried to perfectly catalog his garden's contents was in the 1980s, when there were about two thousand varieties. Keeping exact records ultimately wasn't feasible for a sole gardener, but he nevertheless maintains four long

metal boxes of index cards detailing decades of information—not only the Latin names of particular plants but also notes on their growing preferences, performance, and locations in the garden over time. While it may not be possible to preserve a living collection in the same way he safeguards the treasured household objects his family has lived with for more than a century, his work to document the garden follows the same commitment to preservation.

The two-acre property, which was originally part of the farm's horse pasture, was gradually molded into its current shape over the first half of the twentieth century. The irregular parcel has plenty of curb appeal, but the majority of the garden's treasures are to be found behind the house, beginning at the ancient springhouse that partly gives Hedgleigh Spring its name. Fences, walls, and garden beds exist where they were first built. "Not much of the design has changed," Cresson explains. "I've kept the themes and expanded them." He devotes much thought to maximizing the life span of the specimens planted by his forbears—for example, his grandfather's collection of the shockingly cheerful hybrid evergreen azaleas popular in the mid-twentieth century and the mature trees that create high shade for the rest of the garden. The sole hedge at Hedgleigh Spring is composed of Atlantic white cedar trees. A row of them was planted in the 1920s, and when the trees grew too large in the 1960s, the entire row was cut back. Overriding his instincts to plant

different varieties wherever possible, Cresson later planted Atlantic white cedar seedlings between the original trees to ensure its continued presence in the same location.

A sunken perennial garden, surrounded by a knee-high stone wall topped by a plain white picket fence, contains roses introduced in various decades of the twentieth century, including several ramblers popularized in the 1920s and uncommon in modern gardens. Most of the plants filling out the borders are perennials, such as mature clumps of old-fashioned varieties of garden phlox and rare lilies. Tender plants like salvias and cannas have been added for season-long color and their dramatically scaled foliage. Special varieties of self-sowing annuals like feverfew and opium poppies emerge from seed that has been banked in the soil for decades and can germinate wherever soil is disturbed.

Below the perennial border, an oblong pond is an ideal habitat for both aquatic plants and those that grow on the margins, like Asian skunk cabbage and descendants of the moisture-loving forget-me-nots Cresson's grandfather first planted in the 1930s. A large vegetable garden incorporates many heirloom species of edible plants. Little Crum Creek runs through the bottom of the property, and in the flood plain on the opposite side is a meadow planted with wildflowers and wetland-friendly trees such as swamp cypress.

Even though he is the guardian of the family gardening legacy, Cresson gives himself ample

PRECEDING OVERLEAF: Two differing micro-habitats. The pond allows Cresson to cultivate aquatic and marginal plants, some of which have been there since his grandfather's time. The stone wall behind is the backbone of a dry garden for alpine species.

OPPOSITE: Under an old horse chestnut tree, the garden shed houses meticulously maintained tools that have been in the family for generations.

ABOVE: The backyard rose garden, first built by Cresson's grandfather. While careful to preserve its historic features, the garden today is much more complex and intensively cultivated than in past generations.

latitude to experiment and to increase the garden's focus on the plants that engage him most. He sets the bar high for his garden, demanding four seasons of interest and challenging it to produce something in bloom every day of the year. This requirement has guided his study of camellia shrubs and early- and late-season bulbs. Depending on the species, camellias bloom either in winter to early spring (Camellia oleifera and C. japonica) or in autumn to winter (C. sasanqua). He began experimenting with the species when they were less common in our region and before many of the hardier varieties had been introduced. Now his collection numbers around one hundred plants, many of them mature specimens reaching fifteen feet tall or more. Camellias are promiscuous self-sowers, and he's always looking out for seedlings that may have inherited superior qualities from both parents, possibly making them worthy of commercial release as new cultivars.

Cresson has a particular attraction to other plants that aren't typically thought of as hardy in our region. Besides camellias, he grows two kinds of palms that are native to the southeastern United States. One is a dwarf palmetto variety named McCurtain, after the county in Oklahoma where the northernmost naturally occurring specimen was found. He also likes the needle palm, which can survive Swarthmore winters without protection if it's planted in a sheltered spot. Other somewhat-tender plants he's successfully overwintered outdoors include several types of tropical ginger and two kinds of fuchsia, which have survived long enough to become woody shrubs on a sunny, south-facing terrace sheltered by the house from cold winter winds.

A brick patio is given over entirely to plants either in queue to go into the garden or enjoying a summer outside before being hauled indoors for winter. "There's a little too much clutter here, but unfortunately I can't quite get away from all these interests," Cresson muses while surveying the hundreds of flats, nursery pots, and containers that fill the space. So much is going on here that it's easy to miss a large in-ground banana tree that bears fruit. This plant is usually grown in cold climates as an annual for its tropical foliage. He extends the growing season with a clever hack—sliding a Tyvek-covered frame filled with building insulation over the banana's trunk and, on cold nights, plugging in a heating cable to keep it from freezing. The protection allows the plant to begin actively growing in early spring, giving enough time for the formation of fruit, which in some years is edible.

After a career spent working in public gardens (first in England and later throughout the Philadelphia area), writing books, and teaching for several horticulture programs, Cresson is widely recognized for his horticultural expertise. He is generous about sharing both his knowledge and his garden, which he opens to groups and individuals regularly throughout the year. He's also a profuse plant sharer, happy to gift his visitors with a special iris division or camellia seedling. "All I've ever wanted is a garden that's equivalent to the greatest gardens I've ever visited," he explains. "It's the pursuit itself that is thrilling to me." That he is able to maintain this ambition while also holding true to his family's history is a testament in equal parts to his skill as a plantsman and his familial devotion.

1

2

3

BOTH PAGES: 1. Primula rose. 2. Heirloom Karume rhododendrons, planted by Cresson's grandfather in 1948, and the hardy McCurtain Sabal Palm, named for the county in Oklahoma where it was first discovered. 3. Wild columbine. 4. The rare variegated lily of the valley. 5. Blossoms of a few of Cresson's extensive camellia collection, some of which are varieties he hybridized. 6. Red Dutch oriental lily. 7. Fern fronds undauntedly poking out from the paddles of a hardy flowering cactus.

A MASTERPIECE
INHERITED

Doylestown

In the spring of 2019, Jennifer Bilt and her husband, Steve, were considering relocating to the Philadelphia area from Orange County, California. On a vacation stopover to visit Jennifer's parents in Bucks County, they looked at several nearby properties, none of which felt quite right. On their last morning, a new listing in Doylestown popped up, and they had just enough time to see it before heading to the airport.

For both of them, it was love at first sight.

"This is it," Jennifer remembers thinking when they drove into the cobbled motor court lined with perfectly pruned hornbeams on one side and blossoming cherries on the other. Fortunately, Steve was equally smitten by the property, and they rushed to put in an offer. It was accepted, and they completed their cross-country move later that year.

The old farmhouse, dating to 1752, was built of warm-hued fieldstone and was shielded from the road by a mature evergreen hedge. The property also featured several outbuildings, including a massive wood-and-stucco Pennsylvania bank barn with joists that still bore axe marks from being hand-shaped almost 200 years ago. Most of the original 120 acres had been previously donated to a land trust, leaving the remaining six acres with

preserved views and peaceful surroundings. A modern addition to the house had a wonderful provenance, having been designed and built by the famed woodworker George Nakashima in the 1950s, when the property had been owned by one of his artist friends.

But what struck the Bilts most on their first visit to the property were the extraordinary gardens. They were the culmination of a decade-long project by the previous owners, professional art directors who had used the property as a weekend retreat. The couple had created a variety of extravagantly over-the-top fantasy gardens, which somehow succeeded without compromising the property's integrity or detracting from any of its pleasing simplicity. Although they'd had a vision, both were unschooled in horticulture, so they relied on nurseryman Joey Walter, of Walter's Nursery, to bring their dreams to life. "They would describe a place they had been or a look they wanted and say, 'Just work your magic, Joey,' and I'd have to figure out what they meant," recalls Walter. "It was very difficult, but we developed a great working relationship."

This ten-year collaboration resulted in galleries of gardens designed along a circuit that leads

through the entire property. As a visitor strolls, various vignettes unfold, each complete in itself but relating to the others through glimpses of what's behind and what's ahead. Meanwhile, the strong design forces the guest to fully experience only the present moment. The idea was partly inspired by European gardens in which a private world is revealed only after one passes a threshold, whether an inconspicuous gate or a secret door in a wall.

Completing the circuit through the property takes a surprisingly long time, which is intentional. The stepping stones through a forest of birch trees underplanted with woodland perennials are laid just slightly off-kilter, requiring a slower passage through the space and creating the opportunity to deeply appreciate the tranquility of the landscape. Elsewhere, an out-of-the-way allée of gnarled dwarf crabapples playing off the perfectly mounded forms of Newport Blue boxwoods leads enticingly to a gate below a grove of graceful weeping cherries. Passing through that gate brings a visitor to an English-style garden with more boxwood-lined perennial beds and a series of clematis-wound arches. Everywhere, the gravel for the paths was specifically chosen for the particular crunch it makes underfoot and also for the slightest struggle it creates for one who walks on it—another almost imperceptible cue to slow down and look around.

After heading through a few increasingly naturalistic areas, the visitor ends this multisensory experience at a cluster of garden rooms adjacent to the large barn. Here, old stone walls, clipped hedges, and weathered fences made of vintage tobacco stakes create three distinct spaces. The first is devoted to raised beds for cutting flowers, and the second is a formal parterre garden with segmented beds of tree hydrangeas, low-growing herbs, and rock-garden plants surrounding a table and chairs and overlooked by a riotous backdrop of climbing roses adorning the barn. The last space is an intimate jewel-box garden packed with impeccably maintained perennials, shrubs, and dwarf trees, including several types of Japanese maples and dogwoods. Even the cracks between the bluestone pavers are gardened with intermingling varieties of sedums.

The Bilts feel blessed to live amid so much beauty, especially as their purchase of the property was completed soon before the start of the COVID-19 pandemic. As the outside world became a scary place in ways they never would have imagined, the family took refuge in a six-acre sanctuary where every day something unexpected emerged from the ground, burst into bloom, came into fruit, or otherwise arrayed itself in breathtaking loveliness. Their gardens, designed to reward close observation and encourage contemplation, took on an existential quality as their lives quite suddenly became very small and very private.

Their love for the gardens only strengthened during the pandemic, and it was during this time that they also learned to let go of the initial strain they felt to keep the inherited garden in a

202-203: Before the rest of the garden begins to awaken, cherry trees in the courtyard herald the return of spring. PRECEDING OVERLEAF: A series of arches twined with spring-blooming Clematis montana in a boxwood-lined double border. Although dramatic, materials are carefully kept simple and natural to harmonize with the farm's agrarian past. OPPOSITE: A barn dwarfs an outdoor seating area. No matter the size, relics of the farm's past have been seamlessly incorporated into the overall garden design.

perpetual state of someone else's vision of perfection. The extraordinary creation of which they had become stewards was a complex one, dependent on a schedule of meticulous and intensive maintenance. Its planting had been geared for immediate gratification: Trees installed as mature specimens for maximum impact a decade ago grew to compete with one another for light and space, while hornbeam hedges required regular trimming, hundreds of boxwoods wanted pruning, and flowerbeds needed constant weeding. The couple began to think about what it would be like to make the garden more their own, and a better reflection of their lower-key family lifestyle.

Four years into their tenure as owners and still working with Joey Walter, the Bilts are arriving at a state of balance that preserves the important elements of this horticultural wonderland while allowing their own vision to emerge. They're transitioning a grassy area from being a fruit orchard to a pasture for goats. And Jennifer is growing an increasing number of flowers for cutting and is contemplating the idea of someday making the farm more accessible to garden-loving visitors. "At first we felt a lot of pressure to keep up the masterpiece we had inherited," says Jennifer. But after years spent in close study of the property throughout the seasons—and also coming into her own as a gardener—she embraces the chance for her and Steve to put their stamp on the landscape. "Now I feel really excited about where we can take it from here."

LEFT: A series of garden rooms has been created from what was once a utilitarian barnyard. Here, dwarf flowering Kousa dogwood, Japanese maples, clipped boxwoods, hostas, and ferns surround a relaxing seating area.

PRECEDING OVERLEAF: The massive barn is still the focal point of the farm, and a stunning backdrop for a rustic yet formal garden anchored by four panicle hydrangeas underplanted with beds of cottage-style perennials, all contained within a frame of tidy boxwood hedging. OPPOSITE: A bluebell and Spanish hyacinth-strewn path through a grove of birch trees. The meandering path forces a slower pace and requires one to notice the beauty of the surroundings.
THIS PAGE: 1. Virginia bluebell. 2. Ferns in the birch forest. 3. Siberian squill 4. Unfurling spring foliage 5. Clematis montana. 6. Weathered tobacco stakes are repurposed as fence pickets. 7. Coral Charm peony. 8. Astrantia, a summer-blooming perennial.

PENNSYLVANIA ROOTS

Downington

David Culp speaks with a trace of a Southern accent, acquired from spending part of his childhood in his mother's home state of Tennessee, but his Pennsylvania roots go as far back as the commonwealth itself. His Quaker ancestors arrived with founder William Penn and settled in the 1690s at the village of Germantown, in what is today Northwest Philadelphia. More than 300 years later, Culps still live in the area. David, who lives in Downingtown, Chester County, christened his property Brandywine Cottage when he purchased it in the late 1980s, and he has intensively gardened its two acres ever since.

Back then, this remnant of what was once an eighty-acre farm included a modest white 1790s farmhouse that he likens to a child's drawing for its simple lines, economy of form, and absence of decorative elements. The land was sloped, with the house facing the road halfway down the hillside. A small barn and the ruins of a stable also remained, but aside from some patches of nice hardwood trees, most of the existing plants were either poison ivy, multiflora rose, or Japanese honeysuckle.

Culp is well known in the world of horticulture as a writer, speaker, teacher, and plant expert. He spent much of his career researching new plants, a job that required an almost encyclopedic knowledge of commercially available ornamental varieties in his pursuit of finding new garden-worthy introductions. A committed plantsman, he knew that he wanted to surround the little farmhouse with beautiful gardens that leaned into naturalism and blurred the lines between the hand of the gardener and that of nature—even if executing this vision had to wait for all those vines to be cleared.

He describes himself as a beloved child in an extended family that indulged his interest in the natural world. They were permissive about what he was allowed to bring into the house, although he was taught early to respect all living things. "The rule was if you can take care of it, you can keep it," he remembers fondly. While this philosophy may have originally referred to the turtles and frogs Culp brought back from his outdoor explorations, a reverence for nature has clearly influenced his evolution as a gardener. The cottage-style gardens he and his partner, Michael Alderfer, have created don't try to exactly copy

scenes that occur in nature but do capture something of their spirit by offering a lush habitat for many species of living things. Carefully planned and tended beds and borders hug the lines of the farmhouse, and the spaces and plants become gradually wilder as they creep closer to the property's outer edges.

The centerpiece, located not far from the house, is a vegetable garden surrounded by a waist-high white picket fence. Inside, four beds divided by walking paths are laid out in the traditional Pennsylvania Dutch style. Outside the fence, the pickets act as backdrops for double borders up to fourteen feet deep. The borders contain some of Culp's and Alderfer's favorite ornamental plants, including roses, which climb on posts or have been placed as shrubs, and romantic perennials of yesteryear, such as phlox, lilies, peonies, and irises. New generations of self-sowing plants like poppies, foxgloves, and forget-me-nots emerge each spring, as the gardeners are careful not to suffocate their tiny seeds by overmulching.

These beds, bursting with flowering plants in the spring and summer, are counterbalanced by other gardens placed where they will be appreciated during the colder months. The hillside just above the house's driveway provides the most dramatic of these spaces and functions almost as a plant theater, particularly for Culp's well-known hellebore collection. The bell-shaped flowers of this winter-blooming perennial face down, and

when the plants are grown on a level site, the blooms are hard to appreciate without getting down on all fours. But staging them above eye level on the slope offers a painless and more dignified way to enjoy their subtle variations of color and pattern. This is also where Culp displays many of his hundreds of varieties of snowdrops, which bloom from fall until early spring. The placement of this high-interest garden next to the driveway makes it satisfyingly visible from the window of a warm car on a raw winter day.

The gravel driveway itself doubles as a garden, featuring smaller plants (like corydalis and bulbs such as delicate species tulips) that thrive in the alpine-like dry, rocky conditions and are best viewed up close. Culturally demanding plants—like lady's slipper orchids, which are native to boggy areas of the eastern US—are plentiful in a site next to the house that Culp calls the jewel box garden. Also growing there are his rarest specimens of snowdrops and other ephemeral bulbs. And near the front door, the entrance garden is shaded by large cedars and spruces that create a cathedral effect and a staging area for the couple's many container plants.

A work area that's out of site of the main garden is the fantasy of every small-space gardener. Brandywine Cottage's workspace, which contains a seedling nursery next to a generous composting area, is visually separated from the rest of the garden by a curtain of towering white pines interplanted with Leyland cypress and arborvitae trees.

PRECEDING OVERLEAF: In springtime, the simple, strong structure of the fenced-in vegetable garden and the painted tuteurs are standouts in the garden. Later, these elements will nearly disappear under layers of plants.

OPPOSITE: Spring Green tulips echo the white-and-green bracts of a flowering dogwood. A chartreuse-leaved bleeding heart adds a touch of acid to the display.

ABOVE: The delicate nodding flowers of penstemon, a favorite of pollinators.
RIGHT: Adhering to a geometrical layout and straight lines in the garden's design allows the plants themselves to be the stars of the show.

ABOVE: Some of Culp's special snowdrops. He's careful to label every bulb, as their variations can be subtle. LEFT: An arrangement of Ghislaine de Feligonde roses on the patio. OPPOSITE TOP: A variegated pagoda dogwood in spring. This small native tree also has wonderful fall color. OPPOSITE BELOW: Simplicity is a tenet of the home and garden's design. The plantings are anything but. OVERLEAF LEFT: Looking up into the turning foliage of a redbud tree in fall. OVERLEAF RIGHT: The curious spring flowers of the pawpaw, the largest edible fruit native to the US.

Another distinctive feature on the property is the ruin garden, where hundreds of plants have been coaxed to grow from the two remaining stone walls of a crumbled stable located between the house and the road. Here, pots of spiky agaves, trails of sedum, and antique stone troughs planted with alpine species replace the rusty tools, coils of frayed rope, and coffee cans full of nails typically found in old barns and outbuildings.

Culp, a Quaker, identifies with the long and rich tradition of Quaker gardens. Once the dominant religious sect of southeastern Pennsylvania, early Quakers believed that through close attention, God could be found in every living thing. Understanding the cycles of nature and the interconnecting relationships within the natural world brought one closer to having a direct relationship with God and understanding his intentions for his followers. Quakers also adhered to a practice of extreme simplicity and eschewed any demonstration of gratuitous display. This influence is evident in Culp and Alderfer's garden, where there is an abundance of wonderful plants but very little other ornamentation. The objects placed throughout the landscape, such as old millstones and troughs, were originally created for utilitarian use.

The gardeners' kinship with the earth is perhaps most palpable in the addition of a meadow garden—created in an area that's visually disconnected from the house and the rest of the garden—that is enjoyed by neighbors and passersby on the road. The meadow shows that ecology and aesthetics are not mutually exclusive and that we can create spaces that benefit wildlife and give us beauty while requiring minimal devotion to their care. On this dry, sunny hillside, eastern US species of shrubs like sumacs mingle with grasses, choice cultivars of native perennials such as coreopsis, asters, echinaceas, and penstemons, and plenty of bulbs that add color and texture.

The meadow, like the rest of Culp and Alderfer's garden, is designed to look innate rather than appear as a decorative embellishment on the land. It also personifies the old Pennsylvania Dutch idea of *Gemütlichkeit*. The word defies direct translation but conveys feelings of cozy warmth, peace of mind, and positivity that arise from being at one with your surroundings and sharing that special connection with others.

OPPOSITE: In April, white, pink, and eggplant-hued tulips provide a long-awaited dose of color while the perennial border is otherwise just waking up.

OPPOSITE: Dappled shade creates the perfect setting for an outdoor dining area and is appreciated by some of the many potted plants that spend their summers outdoors. ABOVE LEFT: Double-flowered Anemonella Betty Blake. ABOVE RIGHT: Double-flowered quince, an old-fashioned standby shrub. RIGHT: In a shady area, the white flowering stems of goat's beard mingle with ferns and hostas. OVERLEAF: The walled and secluded ruin garden is a world unto itself.

MAKING HISTORY

Newtown Square

The vision for Marlborough Farm started back in 1993 with the invention of a persona, a common tactic used by marketers to define their ideal customer. The idea was proposed by landscape architect Jonathan Alderson when he was hired by a family (whose members wish to remain unnamed) to reimagine a newly acquired piece of open farmland. Located in Willistown Township in Chester County, Pennsylvania, the land had a long history going back to the Lenni Lenape tribe, on whose footpaths the first roads were laid when Quakers settled the area in the 1690s. The last farmhouse on the property burned down in the 1920s, and except for a row of sculptural white pines separating two fields on the fifty-four-acre tract, other vestiges of its agricultural past have also disappeared over time. A bank barn—named for the vernacular building style in which one long side is banked into a hillside to allow horse-drawn wagons access to the second level—still stood. But the property hadn't been actively tended for decades, and it was now under siege by a slow-moving army of invasive multiflora roses.

Even in this condition, the land seemed special. Its mellow fields glowed in the soft Chester County light, and fringes of mature trees on the perimeters made the modern world feel far away. To help guide their vision and engender a connection to the property's physical location, Alderson suggested creating a backstory for the farm and imagining who might have lived there. Together, he and the family decided that it had been owned long ago by a hardworking farmer who, through a stroke of good fortune, had come into some money. Since this man had simple tastes and was steered by a deep attachment to his land, he had undertaken a series of solid but unpretentious improvements to the landscape and its buildings.

With this bit of whimsical invented history in place, a plan for the farm began to come into focus. One of the advantages of starting from such a blank slate was being able to develop a series of axes and intentional sight lines upon which to lay out the new buildings and emphasize the best views. John Milner Architects, a Chester County firm, was engaged to design the residence and nearby outbuildings. The architects sited the house toward the front of the property and close to the road, both to harmonize with the other similarly situated farmhouses in the vicinity and to maximize vistas of the fields behind. Concurrently, work began to design an

appropriate garden. Most landscape plans need to accommodate existing roads, walls, and grade changes, but in this case, recalls Alderson, "We were able to work out the ideal spatial relationships first and then create the infrastructure."

At first the house was a small two-story farmhouse with one bedroom. Later, two additions were constructed as the family transitioned from using the property for weekend respites to a full-time residence with space for guests and entertaining large groups. Today the house features asymmetrical massing and broken rooflines, with eaves extended to different lengths in the style of traditional farmhouse architecture. While some of the building stones were quarried, others were plucked from the property's fields to provide an exact match with the material of the existing barn.

The garden, like the home, avoids rigid symmetry and was established to take advantage of sight lines to the most beautiful scenes. A gravel cartway runs just below a long retaining wall and was designed to appear ancient. Here, the grass was planted to look worn down from centuries of imaginary horse-drawn wagons passing from the fields to the stable and to several barns housing farm equipment and the family's pet goats, sheep, donkeys, and cows. Along the cartway, successive gardens are laid out in a linear fashion. Closest to the house is a meadow garden under the high canopy of two oak trees. Tall warm-season grasses and swaying native perennials create a sense of constant motion that's in contrast to stationary

features like antique stone pillars placed throughout the area and a formal, clipped Parrotia persica (Persian ironwood) hedge beyond. A break in the hedge reveals a magical walled garden, envisioned as a space the farmer would have planted for his family's enjoyment. Four rectangular beds are arranged around a central millstone water feature in this garden, where sheared boxwood balls frame the mixed perennial beds filled with flowering plants, including peonies, irises, lilies, and roses that would have been found in the farmyards of eras past. Four craggy specimens of dwarf crabapple—a farmyard staple—anchor the beds and add structural interest, invoking formality but not pretentiousness.

Beyond the busyness of the formal garden lies another, more contemplative space: a simple planting of two apples trees and a few perennials surrounded by more hedging tall enough to screen the farm's activity. Here, a potting shed (next to an attached greenhouse) is outfitted with two rocking chairs and overlooks a calm rectangular pool in the center of the lawn, providing a good place to enjoy the reflection of the sky and perhaps one's own thoughts.

Down by the old bank barn, a walled vegetable garden contains functional raised beds and a fence line of espaliered apple trees. Ancient-looking stone walls serve modern purposes, such as hiding utilities. A small stone outbuilding was whitewashed and then later had some of the coating removed, leaving flecks of white pigment on

PRECEDING OVERLEAF: The traditional architecture of the home is extended to the driveways and paths, with all elements designed to appear as if they were created centuries, not decades, ago.

OPPOSITE: Thoughtful attention is paid to every corner of the elegantly rustic garden rooms. Here, traditional farmhouse garden plants like bearded iris and flowering crabapple contrast with the deep red foliage of a flowering plum.

its stone walls, elongating one's impression of the farm's history.

After spending time in the garden at Marlborough Farm, a visitor may begin to almost feel like they have landed a bit part in a romantic play that extols the rewards of rural life. So many of the elements here—the weathered red paint on the barns, the old-fashioned plants in the landscape, and the stone walls given a convincing patina of age with a coating of manure mixed with yogurt—represent theater of the most subtle kind. And, like the best theater, this garden allows one to be transported to another time and place, if just for a moment.

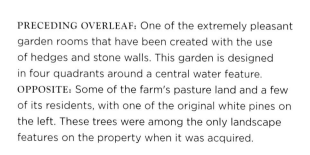

PRECEDING OVERLEAF: One of the extremely pleasant garden rooms that have been created with the use of hedges and stone walls. This garden is designed in four quadrants around a central water feature.
OPPOSITE: Some of the farm's pasture land and a few of its residents, with one of the original white pines on the left. These trees were among the only landscape features on the property when it was acquired.

ABOVE: The covered seating area next to a small greenhouse is one of the most intimate spaces in the garden. OPPOSITE: Long views into the distance allow visibility of the soft contours of the land in this section of Chester County. OVERLEAF: The ancient-looking cartway runs below the garden. The mass of the old stone columns and urns contrasts with the movement of warm-season grasses.

EBB
AND FLOW

Swarthmore

Change, whether it's slow moving or sudden, is elemental to nature. Clearings appear in a forest and then get closed in again. Riverbanks recontour themselves, and pebbles work their way to the shoreline before tumbling back into the water. But what is delightful in nature can be harder to embrace when it happens in our own gardens. When years of work are erased in a day or a season, demoting a beautifully mature space into a problem area, it can be difficult to remain sanguine. Few of us have the zeal (or frankly the energy) to honestly welcome changes created by forces much stronger and more important than ourselves.

Andrew Bunting is one of those rare people who is truly happy to garden at the mercy of the unknown. The work he's done on his suburban plot in Swarthmore, Delaware County, for more than twenty years invites comparisons to a dramatic musical score, with spaces either building toward a crescendo or descending from one. The property is a straightforward rectangular plot of level ground containing a modest two-story cottage built of local stone. Every area has been reworked multiple times, each evolution informed by Bunting's travels around the world and

experiences working at some of the most significant private and public gardens in the US and abroad. Except for one out-of-character Cancún getaway in the mid-2000s, every one of his vacations has been centered on seeing gardens. More recently, a job opportunity in the Midwest led to his absence from Swarthmore for five years, which also had a major impact on the garden.

The house is sited close to the street, so the backyard has far more space than the front yard. In the back, Bunting initially envisioned a series of garden rooms, with the neighboring houses hidden by a ring of evergreens. An early formal bed was inspired by the famous long border at England's Great Dixter garden and consisted of a backdrop of European hornbeam trees, a shorter boxwood hedge in front, and colorful perennials in between. It was perfect until the hornbeams succumbed to disease. Today the border relies less on perennials and more on woody plants for structure. These are combined with lush plantings of annuals and tropicals that provide brilliant color throughout the season. As curator of plants at the Scott Arboretum of Swarthmore College for twenty-two years, Bunting amassed an encyclopedic knowledge of the rarest species, but despite

this, he's no plant snob. This bed contains common plants like coleus, salvias, and cannas, which weave themselves into a vivid tapestry by midsummer. Gargantuan elephant ears and the four-foot-long leaves of tropical banana plants provide a statuesque contrast for the spiky blue foliage of the tender Bismarck palms nearby.

A generous and enthusiastic entertainer, Bunting had long eyed his backyard's nondescript detached garage as a potential place to host indoor-outdoor gatherings. In the early 2010s, he had it renovated into a summerhouse, or more precisely a belvedere (which he subsequently named his garden), a structure designed to take advantage of the surrounding beautiful scenery and which he filled with comfortable furniture accented by the artwork he had collected over time. He gravitates toward the work of artists from the American Arts and Crafts movement, with its emphasis on decorative motifs from nature as well as the blurred line between inside and out. The collector's sensibility evident in the summerhouse's decor is also apparent throughout the garden, where found objects are arranged with natural elements and container plants to create miniature tableaus.

Bunting employed his expansionist tendencies next for a large vegetable garden created after his neighbors accepted an unconventional proposition: In exchange for the use of a section of their backyard, he would design, install, plant, and maintain a garden from which they could all harvest produce. Four large parterres intersected by gravel pathways were built, with one generous section set aside for composting, and another for a chicken coop and run. The space is a true secret garden, entered from a single gate in a long, clipped arborvitae hedge. It was spectacular, but eventually the increasing shade cast by four persimmon trees cut into the garden's productivity. Today the space awaits its next chapter, perhaps as a play garden for the neighbors' young grandchildren.

The front garden has been through several major transformations. It has always been an expression of Bunting's evolving horticultural interests, as well as a response to his environmental concerns. When he bought the property in 2000, there were no ornamental plantings, and the house's symmetry was reinforced by a straight path from the street to the front door. In the front garden's first iteration, he broke the constricting straight lines and planes by installing a nonlinear flagstone walkway featuring an oval-shaped landing with enough space for a seating area (one of many throughout the property). The first plantings were inspired by his time in England working alongside some of the country's greatest gardeners. His skillful interpretation of a cottage garden complemented the home's style and used repeating masses of perennials such as Geranium Johnson's Blue, lady's mantles, gauras, and centaureas—plants that looked English but were also tough enough to thrive in the drier and much

PRECEDING OVERLEAF: The cottage's simple lines contrast the garden's maximalism. The small patch of lawn creates an important quiet moment in an otherwise highly dynamic landscape.

OPPOSITE: The spoke-like foliage of Bismark palms punch up the interest in this mixed bed of annuals, tropicals, and bulbs, while the clipped yew stabilizes this exuberant combination.

hotter summers of the US. It looked amazing, but within five years, the Japanese maple that had anchored the planting died and some of the perennials petered out.

The next iteration was more tethered to the American landscape tradition and included naturalistic swaths of native ornamental grasses, like molinias, and prairie plants, like amsonias, echinaceas, and bee balms. He added some shrubs for structure and winter interest, interspersing the perennials with Limelight hydrangea, winterberry holly, and Asian spicebush. Purple alliums provided fireworks of color every spring. This planting too was gorgeous—until it wasn't.

When Bunting left for his five-year professional sojourn to the Midwest, the grasses became enormous, a cause of distress to the mailman who fought his way through the dewy clumps every day. Deer became more frequent visitors, and the unfenced front was now their tasting menu. Upon his return east, he decided it was time for another change. Inspired by the Midwestern

gravel gardens he had seen, particularly those by designer Jeff Epping, he removed most of the front plantings and replaced the first several inches of soil with gravel. Plants requiring very sharp drainage (and therefore rarely seen in the region) were brought in and planted with their roots exposed. The theory was that the bare roots would reach down through the stone to find the soil below while weed seeds would gain no purchase in the soilless gravel above.

The gravel garden will take several years to fill in and along the way will provide lots of opportunities to experiment. For a while, Bunting will have the fun of being a novice gardener again, trying new plants, such as hardy cacti, unusual lavenders, and even tender agaves, which will need to be dug up and brought inside each fall. He finds it invigorating to be challenged by the complexity of growing plants. If those plants work out, great. If they don't, he'll roll up his sleeves, roll with the changes, and relish the chance to create something even greater.

OPPOSITE: Bunting's interest in tropical plants and succulents as well as his art for arranging is evident on the patio, as is his standards for immaculate presentation, honed by decades of working at public gardens.

ABOVE: Two of the quirky collections Bunting has amassed in his travels find a home in the garden.

OPPOSITE: Color, texture, and form. The three elements are in constant conversation as this garden continues to evolve.

MAIN LINE MEETS CALIFORNIA MODERN

Gladwyne

In the midst of a lengthy and frustrating real estate search, Steve Lyons and Jasmin Fung decided to switch tactics. Instead of prioritizing the house of their dreams—a contemporary somewhere on the Main Line—they shifted their focus to finding a beautiful property. While a structure could be modified, they reasoned, the land and location were fixed entities. And it was indeed the landscape that drew them to the property they ultimately purchased in Gladwyne. The 1950s hillside two-story rancher may not have reflected their personal taste, but the land was lovely: two acres on a south-facing slope, with long views of mature trees. A stream running along the bottom of the property had, in an earlier era, been dammed to create a charming, petite pond that had a fairy-tale-like island at the center.

When they first moved in, they didn't imagine that for the next ten years the property around the house would serve primarily as a staging area for a series of renovations that would completely transform the structure into a contemporary California-style home, a design characterized by the integration of architecture with nature and a blurring of boundaries between the indoors and outdoors. The home's original small windows under overhanging eaves were replaced with wide spans of floor-to-ceiling glass, and interior walls were removed to allow for open sight lines to the outdoors.

Unfortunately, the vistas that had been opened consisted mainly of tall weeds and piles of dirt, as most of the original landscaping had succumbed during the renovation years (when the couple was concurrently occupied with the arrival of two children). Besides the mature trees on the property lines, just a few specimen trees remained, including a Black Dragon cryptomeria and a Sango-kaku coral bark Japanese maple. Having successfully connected their home with the outdoors, it was now imperative to raise the caliber of the landscape.

The first phase was to create level areas to make the space more usable and manage the water that washed down the hillside during heavy rains. Studio Bryan Hanes was engaged to construct a series of terraces descending below the southern face of the house, with the soil retained by Corten steel, a material popular for its durability and attractive weathering over time. The terraced areas, which were also designed to slow the sluice of water during storms, were intersected

by stepped gravel pathways that take an indirect route to the bottom of the slope, encouraging those passing through to slow down and experience the sensory aspects of the gardens.

With the hardscape in place, landscape designer Donald Pell was hired to work on the planting design. Known for his interpretation of the New American Garden style, Pell's work draws heavily on natural landscapes of the United States, particularly the prairie. He takes cues from nature to select plants that have evolved to thrive in the types of soils and exposures he encounters on his projects.

As often happens in construction, the soil profile changed during the renovation process. Instead of having more-fertile layers on top and less-fertile layers below the first foot or so, the ground had gotten churned into an "urban mix" of disturbed particles. Before planting anything, Pell worked on the soil to open up its structure, add the appropriate level of organic matter, and reactivate its natural biology.

Choosing the plant palette was the next step in the process. The homeowners admired naturalistic planting schemes like those of the Dutch garden designer Piet Oudolf and the "new perennial movement" associated with his work, in which large swaths of perennials are intermingled with ornamental grasses. Striking a balance between a wild garden and one that felt under control was the focus of early conversations with Pell, and gradually he created a plant list that

considered a variety of factors: the soil, the garden's slope and full-sun exposure, a manageable level of maintenance, and even the fact that the steel retaining walls produce ambient heat that not all plants can tolerate.

Pell chose plants that, while beautiful, don't look overly cultivated, and he sited them precisely to get the desired performance. As the garden has filled in, he occasionally tweaks the plantings, like a tailor making tiny nips and tucks to get the perfect fit on a bespoke jacket. His adjustments give some plants a bit of extra advantage—such as mulching alliums with gravel so the bulbs won't rot in winter—and act to pump the brakes for others—for example, moving a compact Joe Pye weed, a lowland plant, to a drier part of the garden so it won't reseed quite so much. The goal is to create a balanced system, one that has the right proportion of cool-season and warm-season species to maintain visual interest throughout the year and cover the soil at different growing periods so both early- and late-emerging weeds are kept to a minimum and mulch is unnecessary. While the final appearance is meant to look effortless, much study goes into approximating plant communities that in nature can take thousands of years to establish.

While many of the plants in the garden are natives, some are cosmopolitan visitors. Bulbs such as alliums, fritillarias, and daffodils complement the early-season native golden Alexander. Later in the season, European plants like globe

PRECEDING OVERLEAF: A naturalistic plant palette captures light and movement against the clean lines of the home's remodeled design. The Corten steel retaining panels terrace the steep slope and also slow stormwater as it descends to the creek below.

OPPOSITE: The flowering seed heads of feather reed grass stand erect while the foliage of moor grass softens the juncture of the walkway with the garden beds. Native perennials add pops of color and additional texture to the scheme.

thistle and acanthus fraternize well with native grasses and perennials including bee balm and coneflower. Throughout the garden, cool-season grasses (such as Calamagrostis and Deschampsia species) flower in late spring and summer, while warm-season grasses (including Panicum, Sporobolus, and Molinia species) flower later and look beautiful even in their dormant winter shades of russet and brown. In the front of the borders, various species of catmint create a billowy softness that offsets the strong forms of the larger perennials and grasses.

The gradual rebalancing of the natural systems in the garden is a reflection of trust built over time between the homeowners and their designer. When Pell would at times advocate for a bit more drama, height, or structure in the garden, Fung and Lyons would either stretch a bit outside of their comfort zone (the bad memories of those tall weeds were still fresh, after all) or push back on plants they worried might run too

freely. The result is a garden that combines the science-based design of Pell's approach with forms and colors the homeowners love.

The newly improved outdoor spaces, coupled with the California-modern lifestyle encouraged by their home's renovations, draw the family outdoors for much of the year, both to work—Fung has become a serious gardener—and to relax. The children love the insects, hummingbirds, and other animal life the plants attract (even snakes now hold a fascination). New gardens are being planted at the outer reaches of the property, enticing the family to extend their forays further into the landscape. The children do sometimes ask why their garden doesn't look like the suburban lawns of their friends, but by living amid such a vibrantly healthy ecosystem, they are learning the valuable lesson that even though sometimes the grass can appear greener elsewhere, this isn't necessarily a benefit—in gardens or in life.

PRECEDING OVERLEAF: Coneflowers are the stars of this dense planting, which also includes feather reed grass and great burnet. OPPOSITE: Access to the lower portion of the sloped property is via a system of offset gravel paths and steps. Along the way, there are many places to stop and admire the variation in plantings as well as the abundance of wildlife that is attracted to the garden. Summer-blooming alliums are a favorite of pollinators.

OPPOSITE: It may not offer a view of the Pacific Ocean, but this outdoor seating area exemplifies the indoor–outdoor ethos of California Modernism.

THE ELEMENTS OF STYLE

Chestnut Hill

Once upon a time, back in 1978, a young and energetic couple named Richard and Alice Farley purchased a piece of land in the Chestnut Hill neighborhood of Philadelphia to pursue their dreams of building a home and garden for the family they were looking forward to creating. He was an architect, and she was a landscape architect. Both were eager to harness their talents and passions to produce something unique.

Although the land was unimproved, it—like most places in Philadelphia—had a known history, first as a sliver of a huge estate and then as part of a country club golf course. By the time they purchased the property, it had been colonized by a thicket of Ailanthus altissima, or tree of heaven. Alice urgently set to work clearing the land of the noxious weed tree and filling dumpsters with it, all while pregnant with their first child; Richard began designing their future home in a modernist style.

Nearly a half century later, the Farleys' grandchildren now have free range over the garden that Alice continues to devote untold hours working on—and even more time thinking about. A property that had once been overrun with invasives is now an aesthetically and physically well-anchored hillside garden that has surpassed even her most idealistic youthful vision of what this landscape could become.

Alice is extremely firm in her commitment to ecologically sound gardening techniques, but equally insistent that her designs be practical and the aesthetics never compromised. Over the decades, she has developed these sometimes-conflicting, wide-ranging priorities into a style of gardening that features dense plantings of evenly mixed Asian and native species, with an emphasis on rare trees and shrubs—all maintained using environmentally sensitive methods.

Visually, the clean lines of the house take a back seat to the extravagantly lush gardens that surround it and connect via steps and paths to the Wissahickon Valley Park below. The viewsheds from inside were designed to maximize the link between indoors and out, necessitating consideration of the garden's winter interest. Alice notes that, unlike their Asian counterparts, relatively few North American species of trees and shrubs are evergreen, and because she finds a brown landscape in winter dispiriting, she employs plants from Asia that thrive in the mid-Atlantic climate to add year-round appeal without a lot of fuss.

But she is diligent about including North American species that support wildlife. The property is too small for big sweeps of native plants in the New American Garden style, so instead she tucks native perennials here and there, oftentimes behind showier exotic specimens. This surreptitious planting also allows her to indulge in what she laughingly refers to as her Achilles' heel: planting "drifts of one," an occupational hazard of a true plant collector. "It's a bad habit, but I've never met an interesting, rare plant that I didn't love and feel the need to acquire," she explains. The ultimate example may be her five Idesia polycarpa (you haven't heard of it) plants that could be the largest collection in the US. She scoured the country to find seven tiny saplings of this deciduous Asian tree, and the five survivors bear red fruits in the fall.

Given the steep topography of the property and lack of egress to most of it, Alice relies on a wheelbarrow to haul plants, mulch, and rocks. For decades and by herself, she has spread forty yards of mulch on the garden every year, and the organic material has made the garden's soil—which she now compares to chocolate cake in consistency—very fertile. She doesn't typically use fertilizer but ensures that all the leaves that fall on the property get recycled back into the soil.

To reduce the amount of work needed to maintain the property, Alice depends on extremely dense plantings to outcompete weeds. She has mastered the art of layering groundcovers, perennials, shrubs, and trees, creating an almost baroque complexity of size and scale. Intensive planting also slows the flow of stormwater downhill into the creek below during heavy rains. To further mitigate runoff, she designed the one seemingly flat area of lawn to be imperceptibly concave; a slight depression allows water to percolate before being drawn up by the roots of the overhead tree canopy.

Mature trees, some of which she planted decades ago, block enough sunlight to require shade-tolerant plants underneath, so species of hydrangeas, rhododendrons, daphnes, pierises, and camellias all feature prominently. She has collected nearly twenty varieties of flowering dogwoods, many of them variegated. But since a shade garden will never be intensely colorful, especially once spring has passed, she exploits texture and various hues of green, from chartreuse to bluish, to generate visual interest throughout the summer. Her technique of planting tightly results in borders that are vertically dense and virtually stacked. Some beds are anchored in front by dwarf conifers, which provide another textural element. The green shades of the garden blend seamlessly with the wooded Wissahickon Valley Park below.

The original views into the valley have been blocked as trees have grown up, but new vistas have opened up, often through traumatic events. In 2020, just weeks before their daughter's garden wedding, a windstorm swept through the Farleys'

PRECEDING OVERLEAF: Stairs have been constructed throughout the sloped rear of the property, often built by Alice herself with stones she's pulled from the earth. Intersecting pathways create several circuits, which allow visitors to appreciate the entirety of the densely planted garden. OPPOSITE: The fall-blooming September Charm anemone in closeup view.

garden, wrenching some of the largest trees out by their roots and leaving fifteen-foot-deep holes and a mangled garden in its wake. In search of an immediate fix, the Farleys had concrete rubble hauled in to partially fill the yawning depressions before bringing in load after load of new soil to level the ground. When the wedding day arrived, the garden was beautiful, and the event was a success. Later, the Farleys even learned to appreciate the reemergence of long views into the valley.

In her career designing gardens for homeowners, Alice offers counsel based not just on what she's learned academically but also through her own life as a gardener. When people want to make a garden more environmentally friendly, she encourages them to take baby steps, especially if they are unsure about how to proceed. You don't have to rip out a mature bank of nonnative azaleas, but maybe take up a few square feet of lawn and plant native perennials in that space, she suggests. She also asserts that it's possible to have a beautiful garden that is practical as well by building the soil, choosing plants carefully, and planting them closely. Lastly, she offers this somewhat paradoxical advice: Don't be in a hurry to achieve your dream garden, but be swift to embrace change when it comes.

OPPOSITE: A shady corner is brightened by the foliage of chartreuse hakone grass and a yellow tree peony amidst boxwood and perennial groundcovers.

ABOVE: Dense planting is a strategy for lowering the maintenance requirements, as weeds are outcompeted. Here, hosta, maidenhair fern, Virginia bluebell, and epimedium grow literally on top of one another.

PRECEDING OVERLEAF: Because the home was designed with views of the garden in mind, Alice makes abundant use of evergreen plants to keep the garden interesting even in winter. Hollies are a favorite, as are nandina, cryptomeria, and rare rhododendrons. OPPOSITE: The exceedingly rare Idesia tree in fruit. THIS PAGE: 1. A shady place to enjoy the garden. 2. The terrifying stems of a contorted hardy orange tree. 3. Lilac in bloom. 4. Japanese jack in the pulpit, one of many Asian species Alice admires, although natives also have strong representation in the garden. 5. New growth on a variegated evergreen osmanthus. 6. One of several garden statues placed throughout the garden. 7. The buds of pieris, another evergreen shrub. 8. Stone columns add some flair to a mixed shrub planting.

RIGHT: Perennials and shrubs are intentionally stacked, with lower plants in the forefront. Multistemmed river birches provide shade and interesting bark all year long.

THE
COUNTRY LIFE

Newtown Square

Willistown Township, in Chester County, Pennsylvania, has been a farming community since at least the early eighteenth century, when the landscape was dotted with the fields and buildings of largely self-sufficient family farms. Most produced enough fruits and vegetables to feed an extended clan and to take to market. They raised animals such as horses, pigs, sheep, cows, and chickens (as well as the grain and hay to feed them) and made processed items like butter to sell in Philadelphia. The size of these farms would grow or shrink based on the size and makeup of the families, and over time they evolved into properties with no obvious boundaries and often contained multiple farmhouses.

In the early twentieth century, many farms and estates on the Main Line—which was closer to Philadelphia than Willistown was—were being developed into suburban villas to satisfy a growing middle class. Devotees of the pleasures of country life, particularly foxhunting, found themselves without enough open space to enjoy their sporting pursuits. In foxhunting, riders follow a pack of hounds tracking the scent of a fox, an activity that requires vast amounts of open yet maintained space in addition to congenial relationships with farmers whose land the hunt passes through. With its location beyond the city suburbs, Chester County still retained its rural character, and the open farmland and rolling hills were both beautiful and favorable for riding. Within a few decades, many old farms here were acquired as riding properties to be used by Philadelphians during the foxhunting season and on weekends. This new wave of owners—sporting people rather than farmers—largely preserved the vernacular Pennsylvania farmhouse architecture while adding gardens, swimming pools, and tennis courts to enhance the recreational features of the properties.

Today, the area is still attractive to those who appreciate country life, especially equestrians. Kirkwood Hall, located in Willistown Township on land used by Radnor Hunt—one of the largest remaining hunt clubs in southeastern Pennsylvania—exemplifies the tradition of this section of Chester County. The owners and their family, who wish not to be named, have a deep reverence for the property's history and traditions and have created a very modern working farm that draws heavily on the region's past. A large portion of its hundreds of acres is dedicated to

pasture for the family's event and hunt horses, and more space is reserved for grazing cows, goats, and sheep, foraging pigs, and cultivated orchards and gardens.

When the family arrived in the early 2010s, the farm hadn't been given much recent love. The buildings needed restoration, the property lacked adequate infrastructure like roads and fence lines, and the field overlooked by the farmhouse was poorly drained and swampy. The landscape was beautiful, but two statuesque copper beech trees and a few remnants of shrubbery near the house were all that remained of what had most likely been a simple farmhouse garden many decades ago.

Built of local fieldstone, the house has simple lines devoid of ornamentation and sits close to the road in the manner of many eighteenth- and nineteenth-century farmhouses. The original entrance is a vestige of an era when people traveled along narrow country lanes on foot or on horseback, as the road has no shoulder for parking. A straight walkway flanked by an old Japanese holly hedge bridges the short distance from the road to the front door. Visitors today must come by car and access the house from one of two parking areas. So the first round of gardening efforts focused around making these approaches more welcoming, including widening the original narrow paths and steps and adding boxwood edging as a visual aid for wayfinding. A woodland garden was created under the one remaining ancient beech (its companion having succumbed to old age), whose shallow roots

had suffered under decades of mowing. Instead of grass, the area is now carpeted with spring ephemerals followed by shade-loving perennials. Several river birches create a canopy over the irregularly shaped flagstone walkway that curves toward the side porch, and a hornbeam hedge separates the woodland from the open spaces beyond.

The family's approach to other landscape improvements respects the farm's quirks and tries to preserve historical layers while adding new elements to increase its beauty and livability. Although active farming operations were relocated away from the house long ago, a number of low stone farmyard walls and building foundations still stand, and the home looks out at gardens that have been planted within and around them. At first glance the landscape is a bit hard to decipher. But as it comes into focus, one can see that the palimpsest of walled gardens, long panels of grass, boxwood hedges, and mixed perennial and shrub borders are growing inside or along the foundations of buildings gone for so long that no one knows exactly what they would have been.

The largest of these spaces is a partly walled formal garden, bordered on one side by plantings of crape myrtles and Annabelle hydrangeas interspersed with perennials that bloom throughout the season. Here and elsewhere in the garden, classically inspired statuary and garden accents serve as focal points. Many of these were acquired when some of the last grand Main Line estates were broken up and sold off for parts.

PRECEDING OVERLEAF: Beds outlined in bluestone edging are planted with bulbs in spring, followed by annuals for cutting in summer. A wooden pergola helps evoke the feeling of a walled garden.

OPPOSITE: One of the many existing stone walls that have been incorporated into the garden's design. A millstone acquired from a nearby estate was repurposed as a tabletop.

A step down from the formal garden is a boxwood-edged rose garden, and a level below this is a large cutting garden that supplies flowers for use indoors. Configured as rectangular beds organized around a lozenge-shaped central bed, it showcases successive plantings of bulbs and annuals. A pergola draped with wisteria lies at the far end of the cutting garden, creating a shady spot to enjoy beautifully framed views of the fields and pastures beyond. Nearby, a smaller walled area is the perfect size for a secret garden planted by the children in the family every spring in honor of Mother's Day.

Between the formal gardens and the pasture, an ancient icehouse stands near a dammed-up spring, a former animal watering pond that is now mostly silted in. This early alteration to the landscape had over time made the surrounding area too wet for riding or play. The problem was solved by seeding a meadow with warm-season grasses and perennials planted in large bands. The deep roots of these plants soak up enough groundwater to keep the paths between the swaths of meadow dry enough for riding. The meadow has become a haven for songbirds and insects, and its ever-changing colors add interest to an otherwise green viewshed of rolling farmland.

A long, naturalistic riparian garden, bisected by a curving path paved for the children's bike rides, counterbalances the formality of the beds around the house. Here, native perennials such as amsonias, milkweeds, bluestem grasses, goldenrods, baptisias, and asters are planted under moisture-loving swamp cypress trees. To maximize habitat for overwintering pollinators, the perennials aren't cut back at the end of the season. In the spring, thousands of bright daffodils emerge from the pale-colored duff.

The family is committed to improving the farm for its people, animals, and natural systems, and many of their investments are made with an eye to future benefit. No chemicals are used anywhere on the farm, and food scraps, animal waste, and fallen leaves are composted and returned to the soil. Keeping bees is a family pastime, both for honey production and pollinating the orchards.

In many ways today's Kirkwood Hall hews closely to its historic appearance and function, but the farm is managed much differently than it was two hundred years ago. Instead of a family working the land with help from hired hands, a team of gardeners maintains the property, and additional staff members oversee other farm activities, including extensive organic vegetable production which, along with a greenhouse, supplies food for the farm year-round. And while the farm's owners in simpler times would have made alterations to the buildings and landscape according to their needs, conservation easements—as well as the family's commitment to horses and agriculture—ensure that Kirkwood Hall will retain its agrarian ethos far into the future.

PRECEDING OVERLEAF: Autumn in the countryside. The flame-colored fall foliage of a row of crape myrtles stands out against a backdrop of evergreen arborvitae that shield the property from the road behind. Faded hydrangea flowers and purple asters add to the interest. OPPOSITE: Emerging foliage and catkins of a contorted winter hazel shrub.

ABOVE: A mixed border of flowering trees and shrubs interplanted with evergreens and deciduous tree species. RIGHT: A double-flowered hellebore in early spring. OPPOSITE TOP: One of the family's horses grazing in a pasture. OPPOSITE BELOW: Part of hunt country, these pathways are kept clear for riders that sometimes pass through.

RIGHT: In late fall, the tawny grasses of the meadow stand out in the still-green fields. Adding swaths of native grasses and perennials has made the once boggy area usable for walking and riding. The original reason for the construction of many of the farm's low stone walls is lost to time.
OVERLEAF: The scarred trunk of an ancient beech, one of the oldest trees on the property. Removing turf and replacing it with wildflowers and perennials has spared the shallow roots from additional damage by mowers.

THE BIRD BUILDS ITS NEST

Chestnut Hill

Anyone who has ever attempted to build a beautiful garden knows that it is among the most fleeting forms of creative expression. Knee-high weeds can spring up in less than a week, while invasive trees will take root in just one season. A neglected garden, even one that has taken many years of effort to create, can be retaken by nature in a small fraction of that time.

This hard truth is exemplified by an eight-acre Chestnut Hill property built by a pharmaceutical heir in the late 1920s. Designed by the Willing, Sims, and Talbutt firm, the landscape once included a rose garden, water features, carved stone architectural elements, and extensive terracing on the sloped site overlooking the majestic tree line of the Wissahickon Valley. The wife was a talented gardener, and a tantalizing glimpse of how the landscape would have looked can be found in a few glass lantern slides that survive from this era. In one, a fountain gurgles into a pool surrounded by small pots of flowering plants and low, clipped boxwood hedging. Another shows graceful wrought-iron patio furniture appealingly arranged alongside urns and containers on the terraces overlooking broad lawns dotted with specimen trees and shrubs.

But by the time current owners Jeff and Tallulah Regan purchased the property in 1999, there was no indication that the grounds had once been lovely. The previous several owners hadn't been into gardening, and the house had lain vacant for several years prior to the Regans' arrival. The couple encountered dead boxwoods lining a courtyard of broken macadam, and the fountains, walkways, and terraces were buried under deep layers of leaves and debris.

Only after the Regans undertook an initial cleanup of the property did they understand that the landscape was intriguing, with buttressed stone retaining walls built around the house to make areas level enough to be cultivated. These areas were connected by stone steps and winding pathways that overlooked the Wissahickon Valley's treetops. It appeared that several walled areas seemed to have been made for garden rooms, and the Regans dreamed that perhaps something could be done with an old fenced-in tennis court.

But the house, which had been through a previous half-finished renovation that left floors missing and bathrooms unfunctional, was the Regans' immediate priority. Busy with careers and

three small children, they gradually brought the home back to its original elegance.

With this accomplished, in the late 2000s Tallulah began redirecting her attention to the outdoors. As a professional interior designer, she understood how to create aesthetically pleasing, functional, and welcoming spaces and scenes, but working with plants as a medium was entirely new to her. And with such a large space to regain control of, she admits she often jumped into action mode without quite doing the homework first. This trial-and-error approach initially resulted in more error than she would have liked, but she remained undaunted and did not let up on her efforts, even in the face of difficulties, such as dealing with the deer that have taken a constant and heavy toll on the garden.

The first area Tallulah tackled was the expansive entrance courtyard, which was enclosed by high stone walls. She sited a large oval garden bed in the center, which has had various planting schemes over the years, always with an eye to softening the home's French Norman, heavily textured façade. To keep the inside walls from appearing fortress-like, she planted nandina, hydrangeas, roses, and vines against them. The plants add color and texture not only to this outdoor space but also indoors, as Tallulah loves to clip branches and stems for decorative use in the home throughout the seasons. The double front door is surrounded year-round by an abundance of pots in varying sizes and shapes filled with flowering plants and shrubs, establishing a welcoming entrance to offset the home's somewhat restrained elegance.

Hundreds more containers, many of them antiques, are placed in careful compositions around the property. To keep these pots filled and to avoid the chore of replanting them each season, Tallulah relies on perennials and shrubs. Annuals are used with precision to inject color into a container grouping, and she keeps the result unified by primarily using only one type of plant per container.

She makes lavish use of her favorite flowering plants, and it's not unusual for her to add five thousand new daffodils, fifty more peonies, and another twenty roses in one season. Many of the more special flowering plants she grows are started from seed in a greenhouse that dates to the original owners but was only recently made operable again. Tallulah later plants these unusual varieties of flowers in a dedicated (and securely fenced) cutting garden, from which she clips the blooms that supply her indoor arrangements.

But most of her seed-starting efforts are directed at growing edible plants. The old clay tennis court has been transformed into an impressively productive and well-designed vegetable garden. Its tall, attractively weathered chain-link fence is draped with wisteria, mimicking the walled, "secret garden" effect that appears elsewhere on the property. Inside the massive wooden gate, this garden is just as carefully curated as

PRECEDING OVERLEAF: Any vestige of the entrance's original austerity is softened by foundation plantings of shrubs and vines. Containers, many antiques collected in different countries, further create a welcoming effect.

OPPOSITE: Early 20th-century garden fountains were often designed to drain into the watershed instead of recirculating water—not a viable option for today's gardeners.

the more formal ornamental areas. Cozy seating beckons visitors, and assorted planters, troughs, and urns are arranged to showcase herbs and vegetables. A lattice summerhouse provides a focal point, and pumpkin vines scramble up a rustic wooden arbor, forming a foliage-covered tunnel of dangling squash. Tallulah estimates she grows around sixty tomato plants of thirty varieties each year. Her experiments growing foods that both look and taste appealing often succeed (antique varieties of pumpkins) and sometimes fail (pink celery the taste and texture of cardboard). During the growing season, she cooks, freezes, and cans the garden's yield, allowing the family to eat from the harvest most of the year.

When asked if she ever gets overwhelmed with the magnitude of what she's taken on in her garden, Tallulah doesn't hesitate. "Never," she replies, adding that her work ethic comes from

her large Italian family and a personal inclination to be in almost constant motion. She asserts that relaxing in the beautiful, comfortable spaces she's designed is something she rarely does. Instead, she sets her sights on new projects. She just had an area cleared for an orchard, and she next plans to establish a meadow in a scrubby area below the vegetable garden. "I like to think of how my grandparents influenced me to be a gardener and how now I've created a welcoming place for my kids and grandchildren, carrying these layers and ideas forward to the next generation," she says.

It doesn't bother her that her gardening progress is measured in decades rather than months or years. With patience and perseverance, she knows she will ultimately achieve her ultimate vision, a point perfectly illustrated by a favorite French proverb she likes to repeat: *Petit à petit, l'oiseau fait son nid* (Little by little, the bird builds its nest).

PRECEDING OVERLEAF: The Regans installed a round bed in the courtyard's center to create a circular traffic pattern and make the large space more relatable. Its contents are always evolving, but elements like the boxwood stay consistent.

OPPOSITE: A rustic pergola was made by conjoining branches gathered from around the property.
ABOVE: Baby cucumber and pumpkin, two of the vining vegetables that use the pergola for support as they grow.

PRECEDING OVERLEAF: Part of the vegetable garden, showing a seating area beyond the pergola. Wisteria has enveloped the tall chain link fence, creating a visual transition to the woods. OPPOSITE: View Inside the greenhouse, where Tallulah overwinters plants and starts many of the thousands of flower and vegetable seeds she propagates every year.

ABOVE: Flowers, often in antique shades of pink, are
grown for bouquets and arrangements throughout
the house. OPPOSITE: The long patio includes several
sitting and eating areas, as well as many plants grown in
interesting containers of various materials.

OPPOSITE: A variety of baptisia called Pink Lemonade in the courtyard garden. THIS PAGE: 1. Fallen petals underneath an old cherry tree. 2. Chocolate lace flower, a long-lasting favorite for arrangements. 3. A shady corner enlivened with a vintage sphere and pedestal. 4. Native dogwood blooming in late April. 5. An unusual color of the perennial geum. 6. A comfortable place to enjoy the twilit garden. 7. Potted herbs on the patio, used often in Tallulah's vegetable recipes. OVERLEAF: Indestructible stone tiles cover the floor of the home's solarium, which is opened to the outdoors in warmer months. It is the winter home of many of the garden's container plants.

ACKNOWLEDGMENTS

Many individuals generously contributed their time and ideas to bring this book to life.

We thank the horticultural professionals Kayla Fell, Jerry Fritz, Cindy Hall, Carol Long, Jeff Lynch, Laurie Marshall, Paul Meyer, Renny Reynolds, Nina Schneider, Allan Summers, Bill Thomas, Nathan Tuno, Claudia West, and Carrie Wilks for introducing us to some of the wonderful gardens we got to know while working on this project.

Special thanks go to Jonathan Alderson, Mary Butler, Julia Crawford, Richard Ferretti, James Gager, Chuck Gale, Dan Lurie, Donald Pell, Emma Seniuk, Seamus Trull, Joey Walter, and Larry Weaner for sharing their firsthand expertise about specific gardens. Jeff Groff provided insights into a previously unknown history of foxhunting, and Adam Levine, Diana Cobb, and Rive Cadwallader were instrumental in helping with the text.

We thank Madge Baird of Gibbs Smith for championing this project, and the editorial and design team for patiently working with us through many revisions.

Most importantly, this book would not have been possible without the generosity of the homeowners who chronicled their adventures in gardening and trusted us to share their private and very personal spaces with you.

THE AUTHOR

Photo by Constance Mensh

Nicole Juday grew up in rural Illinois and had her first exposure to great horticulture when she came to Philadelphia in the 1990s. Soon thereafter, gardening became the catalyst for a career change and a source of lifelong fascination and learning. Her work includes serving as the rosarian for Wyck House and Garden, the oldest rose garden in the country. Later she managed the renowned program at Barnes Arboretum School in Merion before working in several roles at the Pennsylvania Horticultural Society. She has served on the boards of Awbury Arboretum and Historic Fair Hill. She enjoys writing and speaking about gardens and garden history and tending her own garden in the historic Germantown section of Philadelphia.

THE PHOTOGRAPHER

Photo by Peter Blaikie for Bachrach Photography

Rob Cardillo has been photographing gardens, plants, and the people who love them for over thirty years. He has more than twenty-five books to his credit, including *Private Edens*, *The Private Gardens of South Florida*, *The Art of Gardening*, and *The Layered Garden*. He is a founding partner of Blue Root Media, which produces *Grow*, the award-winning magazine of the Pennsylvania Horticulture Society. His work is also frequently seen in major garden publications and news outlets. Winner of numerous photography awards, he is a member of the GardenComm Hall of Fame. Rob lives and gardens in Ambler, Pennsylvania, near Philadelphia.

First Edition
28 27 26 25 24   5 4 3 2 1

Published by
Gibbs Smith
P.O. Box 667
Layton, Utah 84041
1.800.835.4993 orders
www.gibbs-smith.com

Designed by Rita Sowins/Sowins Design
Printed and bound in China

Gibbs Smith books are printed on either recycled, 100% post-consumer waste, FSC-certified papers or on paper produced from sustainable PEFC-certified forest/controlled wood source. Learn more at www.pefc.org.

Library of Congress Control Number: 2023942691
ISBN: 978-1-4236-6393-5

Additional photo identifications:
On the cover: Native stonework is a universal hallmark of Philadelphia landscape architecture and complements ornamental gardens like this one in Bryn Mawr; "The Philadelphia Story," p. 139.
Page 2: Unusual dwarf conifers in Coatesville; "Nature and Nurture," p. 49.
Pages 4–5: The perfect symmetry of this boxwood and crabapple allée is backgrounded by the sinuous forms of weeping cherries in Doylestown; "Masterpiece Inherited," p. 201.
Page 6: Cottage garden planting at a Doylestown farm; "Masterpiece Inherited," p. 201.
Page 8: A secluded garden room in Newtown Square; "Making History," p. 233.
Back cover: Dogwoods in April bloom in Chestnut Hill; "Ancestors and Architects," p. 79.